What people are saying about …

SAYING YES

"Cindy writes not just as an artist, but as somebody who has actually done the work in the trenches of church ministry. She offers wise guidance to all who want to help artists bless the church."

John Ortberg, author and pastor at
Menlo Park Presbyterian Church

"As a fellow leader serving alongside Cindy West, I have the multifaceted privilege of witnessing the brushstrokes of her journey from a front-row seat. She truly dances to the music of her creativity and breathes into artists. Inviting us into that story, *Saying Yes* is a must-read work of art about artists and the Divine Artist who beckons them. Artists will find in these pages an inspiring mirror that affirms the beauty of their creativity and the vitality of their calling. Church leaders will also discover a practical window through which they will see a vision of who the bride of Christ can become as her artists are enabled to *Say Yes!*"

Matt Heard, senior pastor at Woodmen Valley
Chapel, Colorado Springs, Colorado

"Cindy gives an inspiring call for artists and the church to accept God's invitation of creative collaboration through the honesty and authenticity of her writing and the experience shared from years of faithful service in local ministry. This is a great reminder to value our artists, steward them well, and keep our vision focused on Christ. I love the encouragement to linger at certain moments in the book, ask questions, and think about what God might be saying to me. I can't wait to share this book with my Worship and Arts staff team. It will sit on my shelf for years as a resource and a reminder of why we do what we do."

Rob Howard, pastor of Worship and Arts at
Fellowship Bible Church, Nashville, Tennessee

"I've had the privilege of working with Cindy West for the past few years. In that time, I've come to love her passion for artistic excellence and sincerity. *Saying Yes* is a celebration of the creative souls God has placed within us. I loved this book and I believe it will deeply impact the artists in your ministry."

Danny Oertli, singer, songwriter, and author

"Cindy's vision challenges the reader to look at worship with a fresh perspective. She inspires us to step out of our comfort zone and engage with the Creator, using our gifts as He intended."

Rita Salazar Dickerson, commission
painter and worship artist

"*Saying Yes* changed me—my heart raced and my breath dwindled as I turned the pages. Cindy, masterful producer that she is, has created fertile ground in which the church leader, artist, local congregation, and the Spirit of God can intertwine in a great dance. Let's all join in!"

Tim Tracey, executive director of worship at
Northland Church, Longwood, Florida

"As both an exquisite artist and an accomplished leader herself, Cindy's words sound a call to both camps. To the discouraged, fearful, and often misunderstood artist, she challenges an obedient step forward—gift in hand—and a resounding yes to our place in God's creative design for bringing Him glory. To pastors or ministry leaders uncertain how to effectively weave the contribution of artists into the fabric of their local church, this book serves as both a toolbox and a guide, shining a light upon the path that could very well lead to the most beautiful and impacting expression of worship and ministry of our time. *Saying Yes* stirred my own artistic soul to say yes more fully and deeply than I ever have before and to trust my amazing Creator and King in the process."

Shannon Wexelberg, worship leader,
songwriter, and national recording artist

"I feel privileged to endorse Cindy West's new book, *Saying Yes*. Cindy has such a passion for the arts as it relates to the body of

Christ, and this book will inspire pastors, artists, and many others to join in creative worship of our God."

Dave Dravecky, retired major league pitcher and founder of the Outreach of Hope ministry

"I worked with Cindy West as a guest worship leader for several years and have found this book to be a needed compilation of her vast knowledge and sincere passion for worship and the arts within the blessed community of the church. Cindy's unparalleled experience in this arena combined with her love for God and His Word make this book a must-read for any worshipper, artist, or Christ-follower."

Kelly Minter, worship leader, speaker, and author of *No Other gods*

SAYING YES

accepting God's amazing invitation to artists and the church

By Cindy West

David C. Cook

transforming lives together

SAYING YES
Published by David C. Cook
4050 Lee Vance View
Colorado Springs, CO 80918 U.S.A.

David C. Cook Distribution Canada
55 Woodslee Avenue, Paris, Ontario, Canada N3L 3E5

David C. Cook U.K., Kingsway Communications
Eastbourne, East Sussex BN23 6NT, England

David C. Cook and the graphic circle C logo
are registered trademarks of Cook Communications Ministries.

The Web site addresses recommended throughout this book are offered as a
resource to you. These Web sites are not intended in any way to be or imply an
endorsement on the part of David C. Cook, nor do we vouch for their content.

Unless otherwise indicated, all Scripture quotations are taken from the *Holy Bible, New
International Version®. NIV®*. Copyright © 1973, 1978, 1984 by International Bible
Society. Used by permission of Zondervan. All rights reserved. Scripture quotations
marked NLT are taken from the *Holy Bible, New Living Translation*, copyright © 1996.
Used by permission of Tyndale House Publishers, Inc., Wheaton, Illinois 60189. All rights
reserved; and MSG are taken from *THE MESSAGE*. Copyright © by Eugene H. Peterson
1993, 1994, 1995, 1996, 2000, 2001, 2002. Used by permission of NavPress Publishing
Group. Italics in Scripture quotations have been added by the author for emphasis.

LCCN 2008931908
ISBN 978-1-4347-9998-2

The Team: John Blase, Amy Kiechlin, and Jack Campbell
Cover Design/Images: Luke Flowers
Author's note regarding cover images: Luke Flowers' ability to express visually what artists
sense only viscerally is a rare gift. View his online portfolio at www.lukeflowers.com.

Printed in the United States of America
First Edition 2008

1 2 3 4 5 6 7 8 9 10

063008

To the amazing artists of Woodmen Valley
Chapel's Worship Arts Community:

Your creative energy and passion for
showcasing God's truth and beauty
inspire me on the deepest of levels.
Despite my leadership title,
it has been you who have led me all along.

CONTENTS

ACKNOWLEDGMENTS

I AM DEEPLY indebted to the self-appointed *Saying Yes* prayer team—Dan, Rob, Don, Liz, Mark, Rita, Betsy, Naomi, Julie, Lynn, Carrie, and Mark T. Your intercession during and between sometimes-agonizing writing days meant more to me than you likely know. Your faithfulness literally prayed this book into existence.

Throughout the past decade, second, third, and fourth chances have been graciously given to me by the elders and leaders of Woodmen Valley Chapel while I wrestled to discover my calling. Specifically, thank you, Matt and Doug, for allowing me to stumble, fall, get up, and try, try again when it comes to learning how to lead. Your insights and encouragement have invited me to become an amazed Christ-follower, a humbled artist, and a far better leader than I would have been without you.

Six years ago, I found more than a friend in Don Pape: I found an advocate for the arts and for artists. His passion for creating and sharing messages of transformation has been a great source of encouragement throughout this entire process. Thank you, Don, for championing *Saying Yes* long before I knew its worth.

I am grateful for the David C. Cook family, who caught the vision for this project and its potential value to believer-artists the world over. The process of penning my thoughts this year has helped to clarify my God-given calling, a season of revelation I will always link to your generosity.

God presents his followers with specific people who make us better, who challenge us, who love us well. My life has been and will continually be enriched by my special friendship with

Ashley Wiersma. The past twelve months of dreaming, planning, and writing has only deepened my respect for you, Ash, and for the worthwhile gifts the Artist has placed within you. I am both humbled and grateful for your collaboration on this work of art.

Mom, Dad, Steve, Amber, Jocie, Stacey, David, Matthew, and Lauren, thank you for giving me abundant love, abundant support, and an abundant supply of crayons over the years. The artist's journey isn't always easy to understand, and yet you choose to love me anyway. I adore you all.

FOREWORD
by Margaret Becker

IF YOU CAME to my house, you would see Cindy West's work in my gallery. It's just a hallway, really, the one from my kitchen to my office, but it's filled with art that moves me and is every bit as inspiring as that found in the Louvre.

I have works from indigenous Brazilian tribespeople, a few salvaged Mayan sculptures, a plywood painting of a lady clothed in sausage by a gnomish local painter named Henry, (it makes me laugh), and a three-panel series by Cindy. The triptych expands my mind, warms my heart, and ultimately, gives me pause.

I first met Cindy over an impromptu dinner in Colorado Springs a few years back. The salad course was no sooner delivered than we realized that we share many of the same sensibilities about art and its vital power. It wasn't long after that dinner when she invited me to speak at her church's annual arts retreat.

Well-designed, unlike any other arts retreat I'd ever attended, my first impression was one of brilliance—brilliance and fresh freedom. During that retreat, she invited artists from all disciplines to bring their artwork for display. On an afternoon break, I walked alone through the makeshift gallery and was awed by the scope of work.

Some pieces were exquisite beyond what even trained artists would be able to manage. Some were clever in a quirky way that evoked laughter and delight. Some were simple, almost primitive in their presentation. Then, three-quarters of the way into the exhibit, I came upon three panels featuring a heart in various states. That piece didn't fit any category.

The first photograph was of a heart riddled by roots and veins, dark and angry and completely unhealthy. The next in the series showcased the same heart but gently swathed in a gauzy bandage. The last featured the heart—full, healthy, now pulsating with life and luster. Catching sight of that one, tears involuntarily escaped my eyes, and I caught a sob midcourse. I was punched, emotionally. The panels read like a book—a familiar book. My life story.

Ah, the power of art—Cindy's art, in this case.

Months later on a blustery winter's day, a plain, brown box showed up at my door that bore no return address. Inside were three square packages, and as I unwrapped the first parcel, the same response I'd had at the retreat that solo afternoon came rushing back. I pulled out the sick heart and then the bandaged heart and then the healthy one and thought, *What a good friend.*

The power of art—Cindy's spontaneous gift to me.

It had the same effect in my grayish living room as it did in the aspen-grove-covered retreat center, the fall prior. Tears, loss of breath, thankfulness. Above all, I think, thankfulness. Because if one were to charge for impact, I could not afford the work represented. If one were to charge for benefit—for the spiritual change such visages can usher in—I would go bankrupt in the pursuit of it.

Art—this art, Cindy's art—given out of a life that believes in the power of God-inspired creativity, left me changed, twice at that point, and countless times since, as I've paused, coffee cup in hand, to revisit the experience as it hangs proudly in the place I call home.

I know the power of music. I know the power of performance art. And over the last few decades, I have come to know the power of visual art more clearly.

Cindy West knows it, hands down. And as you ease your way through this book, you will know it too.

As you digest these pages, your creative self will come to the surface of your life, your priorities, your time allotment and shout, "Here I am!"

For too long, art created by Christians has been so judged by other Christians—so damaging, this attempt to homogenize and edit—that artists have retreated into themselves, disheartened, leaving Christ-given expressions anemic.

We serve the ultimate Creator. Is He tame? Is He predictable? Tidy? Knowable, in full? Hardly. Not in this lifetime. Not by we who are trapped here in this set of parentheses called human form, at least. Why, then, do we attribute such miniscule value and apply such great restraint to the expressions of creativity we express "back into" our culture? Are we afraid of God's undomesticated style? His sky-high risk tolerance? His chaotic-yet-somehow-strangely-ordered ways?

I'll never understand the dynamic. Regardless, I refuse to shrink away from the task of creating from my own unique self, from my own place of freedom. You mustn't either.

Much like Queen Esther, who did the unthinkable—a God-inspired act of recklessness that would seem to some an act of treason—my hope is that you also hear your calling clearly, and respond with bravery and elegance. Because we know what that kind of freedom, that kind of dedication brings when it is obviously God-inspired: It brings nothing less than redemption.

May these pages ignite the courage in you to affect us all, to free us, to remind us of God's omnipotence. And may your artistic offerings move people to comfort others, to allow change in themselves, to embrace God.

Inspire us, artist! Inspire us. You, too, are here for such a time as this.

—Margaret Becker
Nashville, TN

NOTE TO THE READER

THROUGHOUT *SAYING YES*, YOU'LL happen upon sections that start with the title "Linger." It's exactly what I hope you'll do each time you see one pop up … *linger* a bit. Take your time, dwell a spell, dare to go a little deeper with whatever content is being explored. (Given the fact that you're an artist, this part probably goes without saying, but if you stumble onto a non-Linger concept that causes you to *wish* you could linger, then by all means … linger away!)

PREFACE

A MAGAZINE CALLED *Last Days* once dedicated an entire publication to a single challenge. The challenge was to the local church, and it was stated like this:

What will you do with the powerful gift of art?

The cover features a painting of four artists, each sitting on the steps leading up to the church's front doors. Clearly, they're on the *outside* of whatever is going on *inside* the church building.

One artist—a thirtyish man in faded blue jeans and worn black boots—has his chin resting on his left fist, his right hand clasped loosely around three paintbrushes. A semipainted portrait on canvas in orange and gold lays at his feet.

To his left is a young videographer grasping a video camera with both hands. Brown dreadlocks appear underneath his red ball cap worn backward. His head is bent downward with eyes that are fixed in some sort of trance.

On the painter's right sits a third artist, a young woman— twenty, twenty-two—dressed in a petal-pink leotard and tiara with pink-laced ballet slippers wound around her slim ankles. Her sinewy legs and gentle hands are posed in a graceful dancer's form.

Sitting in the shadows, almost completely hidden, a fourth artist appears, a young man dressed in a red and white striped shirt, his painted face a dead giveaway that he is a mime.

Different disciplines, but the very same expression made manifest with each countenance: undeniable and complete defeat. As if to further prove the point, their shoulders are slumped, their eyes are downcast, their hope has long since been dashed.

In the mime's peripheral is a window that reveals the goings-on in the sanctuary. A dapper-looking pastor shakes hands with a young man wearing a gray Trueway Seminary sweatshirt. "Welcome to our flock!" his expression cheers. Which explains the sign outside that says that seminary students are the "future of the church."

I happen to agree that we need seminary students in the church, both now and in future days. But not at the expense of the artist. From cover to cover of that *Last Days* magazine, articles beg the local church to embrace artists and, in mutual fashion, artists to embrace the church. Start a gallery, help train those with artistic desires, create an artist support group, make room for musicians, poets, dancers, painters, video and film makers, and actors in your worship services, pray for more Christian art institutions to be raised up—the suggestions go on and on for how to marry creative types with those who believe they are not. Fantastic ideas. God-honoring ideas. Timely ideas. My heart beat fast as I flipped to the inside front page to check the copyright date. This message is exactly what the church—and her artists—needs to hear today!

The year was 1995.

❧

Three months ago, I sat in a meeting with both artists and arts leaders, including renowned abstract-expressionist painter Makoto Fujimura—"MAH-koh," like *taco* with an "m," he begs to be called by those of us who unwittingly butcher Japanese names. Partway through our time together, he boldly asserted that "the [artists] of this creative age are the wedding planners for the wedding feast that is to come." He went so far as to say that artists, of all people, are the ones who "lead the way for reconciliation, humility, and the recovery of hope."

Wedding planners! What a crazy notion. But the more I let it spin around in my brain, the more I resonated with it. Indeed, a wedding feast is coming. And who besides the artist would God tap to orchestrate its song and color and texture and vibe? Who besides the artist would He trust to fashion the bridal gown and prepare the *hors d'oeuvres*?

Who besides the church—the *consummate* bride—would God ask artists to serve?

Last Sunday in our church's weekend service, we sang a worship chorus that leveled me in ten words.

"I see a generation," it began, "rising up to take their place."

From my seat in the sound booth at the church where I work, I stared at each artist on the stage, each artistic person in the pews. I reflected on the artists who have gone before us, creating and innovating and demanding excellence from within the four walls of the church. I wiggled my toes and reminded myself that I am standing on their shoulders—that *all* of today's artists are—and I smiled.

The artists of old I will never meet, and yet they remain my truest heroes. During the great Renaissance from the 1400s to the 1600s a handful of believer-artists were brave enough to break from tradition. They stayed focused on the task at hand—bringing glory to God with their art. They pursued excellence and in the end walked in obedience.

In return, the church invested in their lives. She drew them in and nurtured them. Most in the church understood the far-reaching importance of God-inspired art. They knew in time the artists' gifts could touch the masses for God's glory. The church supported the artist, which led them to mature in their craft and go on to lead the world in art.

It's what is required of us today as well. Leader of artists, you are called to be a catalyst for this remarkable group of individuals. Take their hands, walk the creative journey alongside them, love them, challenge them, and create opportunities where their gifts can be released.

Church leader who, to this point, has relegated artsy types to the cold, stone steps outside, you are called to do something, as well. Embrace the artists who are sitting in your pews longing to find a home. Learn to trust them. Ask their opinions and listen— *really* listen—to the depth of their creative answers. I dream of the day when the church will serve as the front-runner in terms of artistic truth, artistic innovation, and artistic excellence. I hope you do too.

We all—artists, arts leaders, church leaders alike—face a choice. Will we humbly embrace the gifts our Creator has bestowed upon us, and rise—rise like the Spirit of God that is already "arousing us within," as Romans 8:22 (MSG) assures? The time is now for us to decide! The time is now for us to walk through the doors of the church and a with selfless faith, begin the preparations for the wedding feast to come.

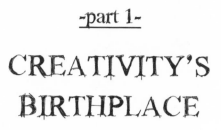

-part 1-

CREATIVITY'S
BIRTHPLACE

-1-
ART THAT MATTERS

Power That Yields Reflection and Engagement

Great art is something that when you experience it,
it lifts you out of yourself, puts you in another dimension,
and places you back down transformed.
—Sister Wendy Beckett

WHEN I WAS in photography school, I took a human-resources job with a large bicycle manufacturer in Dayton, Ohio. It was just to make ends meet, really—I wasn't exactly the HR type. But two days after graduation, the ink still wet on my degree, my boss offered me an interesting role in the firm's training department. As The Huffy Corporation's Service First Video-based Training Producer, I'd be creating videos to help technicians assemble bicycles faster, more safely, and in a manner that would prove vastly more profitable for the company. It would be my first "real job."

Working closely with a scriptwriter and a technical advisor, I began to travel back and forth between Ohio and either California or Michigan, scripting, filming, editing, and mass-producing installment after installment of video-based instruction.

This overall approach to training and development was so cost-effective that Huffy eventually decided to expand the business to include assembly of not only bikes, but also basketball goals, grills, lawn mowers, and even Christmas trees. If you had the piece-parts, we had a drill with a competent technician standing behind it, just raring to go. What's more, because all those drill-happy technicians needed to be trained, I'd basically have job security for decades to come.

The twenty-four months that followed my acceptance of the role were a beautiful blur. I was having a wonderful time creating video after video with a truly terrific team, and although I told myself it was all for a noble cause—that my "art" was doing more than merely boosting the company's bottom line—a deep-seated need within me was going unmet.

CREATING ART THAT MATTERS

During one of the video classes I took in Dayton, an instructor asked each of us to come up with a thirty-second public service announcement video that would be screened for class critique. As I listened to the endless stream of creative ideas flow from the minds of my fellow classmates, I realized I had nothing worthy of presenting. I mean, *nothing.* Zippo!

Two days later, though, I was watching the local evening news when a special report caught my attention. A young mother's two-year-old son had been kidnapped from a nearby store earlier in the week, but new details revealed that the woman had actually lied about the whole deal. There she was on camera, admitting that she had fabricated the abduction story—in fact, she said, she had drowned the boy in the bathtub because he wouldn't quit crying.

I sat back on my couch and experienced the most overwhelming wave of nausea I'd ever known. My stomach did somersaults as I took in the stunned look on everyone's faces. Police officers, news reporters, the woman's family, her neighbors, the entire community—everyone was in a state of disbelief.

As I lay in bed hours later, wide awake with thoughts of this adorable little boy the world would never know, lines of a script formed in my mind's eye. From this tragedy, my video PSA would be born. It would focus on the horrors of child abuse, as told from the perspective, I decided, of a young girl.

Over the next two weeks, I put words down on paper, mocked up children's coloring pictures I'd feature in my video, storyboarded a flow I thought might work, and recorded the words of a friend's young daughter I'd use as voice-over in my school project.

As I scripted, filmed, and edited my piece, I grew more and more nervous about the topic I had chosen. But something inside told me it needed to be done. Abuse needed to be talked about. And it needed to be stopped. Now.

The evening we were to critique each other's work was a jolt to my nerves, to say the least. My classmates presented their PSAs one after another, and with each viewing, it seemed the videos got stronger, more vibrant, and more creative. By the time it was my turn, I was numb from worry.

My instructor slid my tape into the tape deck, (boy, does that date me), and hit Play as someone shut off the lights. I would hold my breath for the entire thirty-second run time of my video.

"Hi, my name is Sarah," said a little girl's voice, "and this is my friend Joey.

"We go to school together. We play ball together. And we *love* to eat ice cream.

"One day," Sarah continued, now with a dose of sadness and softness, "Joey's mom hurt him. She hurt him really bad."

Still softer, "Now, I go to school alone.

"I play ball alone.

"And I never, ever eat ice cream."

After a long pause, the little girl pleaded, "Please stop the hurting.

"Please, stop the pain."

The tape rolled to black, and for what seemed an eternity, no one spoke and no one moved. My entire class just sat silently in the dark, their usual sarcastic remarks held at bay by something akin to reverence that overtook us all. My project had struck a nerve, found a home in people's hearts. But I didn't know that at the time, of course. At the time, I just sat there, nursing my insecurities and deciding that because of my miserable failure, I must never produce another video again.

My self-degradation freefall was abruptly halted by a voice that emerged from the back of the room. "I want to see it again," it said.

Classmates' heads bobbed up and down in agreement as "Yeahs" seemed to arise from every angle.

My instructor approached the VCR stand, rewound the tape, we all watched it one more time, and perfect silence enveloped us yet again. By now, I was in a state of sheer torment. What had I done wrong that they would be left so disturbingly speechless? *Two* times in a row?!

Someone, please say something. Anything!

As the lights came up, I was shocked to see a couple of classmates wiping tears from their cheeks with the backs of their hands. As my eyes adjusted to the light, I looked up to see my instructor staring straight at me. "Cindy," he said, "this was … *powerful.*"

So, while my first two years at Huffy were for the most part stimulating and satisfying, at about month twenty-five, I reflected on that class video project and suddenly knew that helping technicians build better bicycles simply wasn't scratching the itch for me. Instead, I was compelled to create art that would elicit deep and meaningful reflection from people regarding the heart of the human condition: *What is life all about? What am I all about?* And, *Do either of those answers make a difference, anyway?*

These were the questions I wanted people to ask when exposed to the art I'd make. I wanted to create art that stirred people's souls. I wanted to create art that moved people to action. I wanted to create art that really and truly *mattered.*

Art's Question: Will You Enter In?

At some point along the creative process that turns
storyboard-conception into a magnificent work of art,
an unseen question gets carved onto each and every piece:
"Will you enter in?"

It's the question my classmates were asked, at least the ones who were willing to hear it. *Will you enter in?* Into an innocent child's pain? Into the pain of *hundreds of thousands* of children?

It's the same question I hear whispered when I lean in close to a painting in a gallery, when I observe a stellar soprano performance, when I sit slack-jawed, marveling at contestants' contortions on *So, You Think You Can Dance?*

All effective art—all art that matters—wants to know, *Will you enter in?*

You, with your downsides and dark sides and idiosyncrasies.

You, with your failings and flaws.

You, with your busyness and distractions and confusion and aches, your promise and potential and talents and gifts.

You, who are uniquely you.

Will you *enter in?*

It's a profound question to consider, and one I feel sure was at the heart of why I so desperately wanted to be Kelly McGillis from the year 1986 on.

Surely you remember the movie *Top Gun*. In the midst of big hair, Blondie, and the fall of the Berlin Wall, guys like "Maverick," (Tom Cruise), "Iceman," (Val Kilmer), and a gang of their well-conditioned friends proved there was no cooler place on earth to be than the Miramar Naval Air Station in San Diego, California. In the time it took to watch the movie, I had hatched my grand plan: I'd chop off my blonde, curly locks into a shoulder-length bob, buy trendy horn-rimmed glasses, drive an M.G. convertible two-seater around town, and drink water disguised as hemlock all day long, just like Kelly. And just like Kelly, I felt sure I'd attract my own beach-volleyball-playing fighter pilot too.

Admittedly, my motivations for entering into this particular artistic masterpiece were a little less than noble. But that's not true for everyone. They say that after the film's release, recruitment of young men into naval aviation increased by 500 percent. Five *hundred* percent! These were men willing to change the entire course of their lives, and all because of a feature-length film! Secretary of Defense William S. Cohen was asked about the rise in the number of applicants and said in response, "Tom Cruise did more for recruiting than any strategy we've ever come up with."

From another movie seat, I got caught up in the power of history, of story, when I saw *Schindler's List* for the first time. It was the little girl with the red coat that did me in. An all-black-and-white film with a child dressed in red. Who can bear that? When the scene came that revealed her coat lying in a heap of other coats, other bodies, other beings ... bitter tears rolled down my cheeks.

From a theater seat, I have sat motionless during the Broadway production *Cats*, being wrapped deeper and deeper around the story line as Grizabella sang "Memory." The emotion, the candor, the *feeling*—I was mesmerized.

From an oversized seat in my own living room, I have laughed out loud at Anne Lamott's wacky and profound ponderings in books like *Grace (Eventually)*. Her uncanny ability to spit out thoughts we *all* have but are too ashamed to admit makes me cheer her on every time.

More poignantly, from a bench seat at the New York Met, I've had the wind knocked out of me after careening around a corner in the European-influence section and finding a life-size painting titled *The Crucifixion* hanging before me. There, quite literally, I found myself sitting at the foot of the cross, struggling to breathe, trying to take in what it must have felt like to be in the crowd the day Jesus died. All I could do was sit there, eyes lifted, heart bowed at the sight of true forgiveness.

Certain pieces of art have that effect, don't they? They stop you dead in your tracks or catch you completely off guard because somewhere in the secret places of your soul, when confronted with art's power, you see your own reflection there—there in the brushstrokes or the melody or the phrase turned just so. Sort of like hurriedly walking past a mirrored building and being shocked to find yourself rushing by.

Art's power is profound in terms of what it provokes. Maybe it's a burning question you've never had the nerve to ask. Perhaps it's a deep hidden secret that is finding the light of day. Or, as was the case with the abuse video I'd created in school, a calling gets exposed that you're utterly compelled to fulfill.

Regardless, a moment of truth arrives when
we can no longer deny that something profound
is happening around us, to us, inside of us.
Undoubtedly, we are changed.
And the thing called art did the changing.

Art's Promise: Our Own Reflection There

Years before he died, author and Catholic priest Henri Nouwen wrote a short book titled *The Return of the Prodigal Son*, detailing an encounter he had with Rembrandt's painting by the same name. The original hangs at The Hermitage in St. Petersburg, Russia, but evidently the one that so profoundly impacted Nouwen was a sixteenth the size and hung on his friend Simone's office door. The image of a father's embrace that reflected such unconditional love and forgiveness set in motion a "long spiritual adventure"[1] for Nouwen that eventually yielded a completely renovated take on his priestly vocation.

Suddenly, it wasn't just a painting. Suddenly, Nouwen was the son being welcomed home by God, the father with outstretched arms.

Immediately upon laying eyes on the reproduction, Nouwen wanted to know who created it, what they were thinking, and what it was called. The art was that moving to him. "It's beautiful ... more than beautiful," Nouwen would say of the piece. "It makes me want to ... to cry and laugh at the same time.

"I can't tell you what I feel as I look at it," Nouwen
admitted, "but it touches me deeply."

The Return of the Prodigal Son—Rembrandt van Rijn

Years later, still on the spiritual adventure that had been awakened by the painting, Nouwen wrote,

> When I first saw Rembrandt's painting, I was not as
> familiar with the home of God within me as I am now.
> Nevertheless, my intense response to the father's embrace
> of his son told me that I was desperately searching for
> that inner place where I too could be held as safely as

the young man in the painting. At the time, I did not foresee what it would take to come a few steps closer to that place. I am grateful for not having known in advance what God was planning for me. But I am grateful as well for the new place that has been opened in me through all the inner pain.

I have a new vocation now. It is the vocation to speak and write from that place back into the many places of my own and other people's restless lives. I have to kneel before the Father, put my ear against his chest and listen without interruption, to the heartbeat of God. Then, and only then, can I say carefully and very gently what I hear. The painting has become a mysterious window through which I can step into the Kingdom of God.[2]

The life of one man, forever changed by the
power of art. Art that matters.

I had my own impactful encounter with the story of the prodigal son—one of my favorite themes of the gospel message—on a visit last year to Eastbourne, England. I walked through the doors of St. Saviour's Church, a marvelous place of worship that for well over a century has incorporated art into structural architecture so effectively it brings a person to tears.

It had that effect on me, at least.

I stood in silence at the back of the church and let my eyes, my heart, take it all in. The same image of father embracing son that had magnetized Nouwen drew me in. Ignoring everything else, I made my way to the artwork, stood before it, and sighed. Surely this moment in time, this private viewing of a wonderful work of art in an empty and historic church on a glorious Tuesday afternoon was not accidental. Surely, somehow, it had been arranged just for me.

The story was conveyed in a series of brightly colored mosaic tiles, Scripture verses illustrated in an intricate pattern that lined both interior walls. I stood inches from the tiles, reaching up to slowly run my fingers over the tiniest chunks of jagged, colored glass. *Whose fingers first touched what I am now touching? Which artist skillfully chose each piece and carefully laid it in the overall pattern? And how long did it take him to create this masterpiece? Did it ever cross his mind that his work would live well past his own lifetime and serve to impact the heart of another, far less-accomplished artist nearly a hundred and fifty years later?*

I stood there pondering the snappy, instant-everything age in which I live, a time when digital tricks are at every artist's fingertips. (I could "do mosaic" too. In sixty seconds or less, using design-software filters a first-grader could figure out, a click of the mouse, *voila!* instant mosaic.)

Oh, to have lived in a time when art unfolded.

Evolved.

Became.

I walked silently, aimlessly, around the sanctuary's inner perimeter, eyeing the other work and wondering who had been the champion, the visionary mind that possessed enough foresight to ensure that art would feel comfortably at home here, inside this church. I wandered down an aisle and sat for several minutes on the first old wooden pew, eyeing the kneeler at my feet and thinking there just aren't enough kneelers left in the world today. The light danced behind the windows, casting shadows on the colored tiles. *Imagine that. The gospel without words.*

I sat enraptured for the better part of an hour, letting aimless thoughts carry me wherever they wanted to go. Somehow, amid scraped hardwood floors, tattered hymnals resting on dusty book racks, a decidedly ancient scent to the air, the marvelous stained glass, the paintings, the natural light made the whole situation seem anointed. I thought about the masses of people who would come through the doors in just a few days' time—all the preparations that would need to occur between now and then—and I knew somehow I was deeply understood, even all these miles from home. Feeling strangely affirmed and encouraged, lifted up and firm-footed, on my way out, I turned and looked into the silent and majestic space and said, simply, "Thank you."

THE ORIGIN OF POWERFUL ART

If we're walking and talking and living today,
we have the ability—
and the responsibility—to create art that matters,
art that offers up to others the gifts of reflection,
of newness, of actual transformation.

I saw this play out with amazing clarity just yesterday. Of all the art-appreciating seats I've sat in—at a movie theater, in a studio, at the Met—there is a seat that beats all others. It's one I occupy nearly every weekend, right in the middle of the auditorium of the local church where I serve. There, I get to watch firsthand the power of art make direct hits on the human heart time and time again.

As a staff and congregation, our church places a high value on using various art forms to catalyze "God-encounters" during worship services. This past weekend, for example, the congregation entered the worship auditorium to find seven artists onstage, creating already-in-progress masterpieces using only paint and clay.

One artist was painting a powerful image of a large hand holding a small hand, based on a photograph of a grandfather walking with his grandson. He used spade-shaped art knives as brushes, which added increased texture and harsh edges—an interesting juxtaposition to the smooth and tender concept itself.

The unfinished pieces stayed onstage during the sermon, so that people would have time to take them in. During the two closing songs, the artists came back out and finished their work.

Afterward, dozens of people flooded the stage to talk with the artists, but one conversation in particular caught my attention. I overheard a woman sharing how she'd struggled with her father in her past and how the power of the large hand holding the smaller one was almost too much for her to handle. In fact, she could hardly look upon the painting without tears springing to her eyes.

I stood there listening, just marveling at how God was using the image to woo her toward Him, to tell her that He was her true Father, the only one she'd ever need. She was *entering in*. Somewhere during that experience, the Spirit had used a simple art form to move one woman a little further along on her spiritual journey. As I reflect on all that transpired yesterday, I find myself grateful not only for the brief moment of revelation, but for the timeless nature of genuine transformation.

Art that matters—truly great art—shows you more of who you are, or more of who you'd like to become. "Great art," says British art expert Sister Wendy Beckett, "is something that, when experienced lifts you out of yourself, puts you in another dimension, and places you back down transformed." Indeed, it does

Recall a favorite piece of art. What specific details about the art were meaningful to you?

What did "entering in" to that piece of artwork look and feel like for you?

-2-
THE DAY I SAID YES

When God Calls Artists Forth

Your presence is requested ...

I RETURNED HOME recently from two weeks of vacation and was greeted by an eight-inch stack of mail. Most of it was just junk, which caused me to wonder if anyone had missed me during my hiatus besides direct-mail marketers. I flipped through discount coupons, grocery store ads, and five different credit card offers that promised zero-percent financing and every means under the sun of reducing my mortgage. But as I rummaged deeper into the pile, I noticed a cream-colored envelope boasting a dear friend's familiar handwriting. Finally, something worth paying attention to.

I ripped open the envelope and pulled out an engraved wedding invitation laying under a protective rectangle of delicate tissue paper and an RSVP card. *Your presence is requested ...* the invitation began. I scanned the words, noted the date in my mind, and, without a moment's hesitation, reached for the response card to check the little box beside the word "Yes." What an honor to be invited, to have my presence actually *requested*. And especially by someone I cared so much about.

It's true: We get bombarded with invitations to do this or that on a near-daily basis, and most of them *are* just junk. But every once in a while, an invitation surfaces that warrants our time—and our second glance.

> Every once in a while, an invitation comes along
> that is worthy of our yes.

I surrendered my life to Christ at the tender age of thirteen, or "asked Him into my heart" as we said in Southern Baptist circles. On the heels of that decision, I knew I wanted my life to matter. I simply wanted to use my creativity in a way that would move beyond the defenses of the human heart and change it forever. Pretty lofty goal for a young teenager, but somehow, it all made perfect sense to me.

I didn't know how it would play out. What's more, I didn't care. God had fashioned me to be creative, and I just knew He was going to use every imaginative idea and passionate pursuit I'd ever known to somehow bring Him pleasure. The Creator of the universe was extending an invitation to me to come play with Him—to create for His glory and for my own good, and I was fully prepared to say yes. Trouble was, it took me twenty years to actually say it.

MORE THAN ARRIVING

I attended an arts conference about a decade ago, which was not all that unusual an occurrence. Immediately after accepting a role in full-time ministry, I began attending all sorts of conferences dealing with everything from the latest in design technique to how to fire a slacker employee and still remain friends. Or at least friend*ly*. While some of them held my attention, by the afternoon hours, they'd all turn into snoozers. I'd zone out, traveling in my mind's eye to my "happy place," which usually involved a beach and a journal. But at this conference, something was different.

The opening session kicked off with a giant video screen emerging from the floor. Music and lyrics permeated the room as Rich Mullins' voice led us in "Everywhere I Go, I See You." Close-up images of sunflowers and river rocks morphed into vast, wide-open spaces like the Grand Canyon and the cosmos. Morning sun-lighted skies faded to the darkness of night as stars danced to the tempo of Mullins' song. Nature was larger than life, and yet encapsulated in forty feet by twenty feet, on a screen sitting right before my eyes.

God's majesty and creativity was everywhere—there was no escaping it. When the song finished, colored lights flooded beautifully draped fabric as the video screen disappeared into the stage floor. Singers came forward, inviting us to stand and worship our Creator. I'd never experienced anything like it. Brushing tears off my cheeks and yet grinning from ear to ear, I sang with all my heart and found an excitement beginning to well up from deep within me.

> How was it possible to create art that was so powerful that
> it could ease people into a posture of worship this way?

I was mesmerized.

Over the next two and a half days, the audience was introduced to the conference staff team as one by one they shared their journeys as artists and leaders. As each session started, I eagerly anticipated what would unfold. I couldn't wait to worship God through drama, dance, song, video, the spoken word, and Scripture. It felt like a door was swinging wide open, God prodding me to step on through. As each song or screen graphic or stage treatment emerged from the main stage, I'd nudge myself further onto the edge of my seat and whip my gaze toward my teammates. "Can we do *that* back home?!"

They'd shake their heads skeptically, but I knew God was birthing something big inside my farm-girl-from-Missouri dreams.

My friend Dan says that we all start at point A and desire to go somewhere, but life is never merely about *arriving* at point B. It's those in-between moments all along the way—the opportunities that surface, the unexpected pit stops, the lessons we glean at a gas station or on a Kansas interstate or while sitting with an ailing parent—that require our attention, because *everything* we experience is preparing us for our long-awaited destination, wherever that may be. And whenever it shows up.

When I reflect on my own journey, I see all sorts of "along-the-way" experiences—broken relationships, shattered dreams, joy realized, a-ha moments, passion for photography, an awakening interest in video production, a couple of major moves—from Missouri to Ohio to get that photography degree, and then from there to Colorado to scratch my soulish itch to be near mountains. *Everything*—every, single thing—had served to advance me toward this long-awaited destination, which (who knew?) was evidently a stadium seat in a church auditorium at a not-so-boring conference, just so I could finally say yes to God.

YOU HAVE A LOT TO OFFER THIS WORLD

During one session partway through the arts conference, every single artist in the audience was recognized by the speaker who was onstage during that hour. Visual artists, dancers, actors, sound technicians, producers, camera operators, lighting directors, musicians, vocalists, worship leaders, and pastors were called to stand, group by group. And once every group had been prayed for, I found myself wonderfully lost in a moment of gratitude for God's gracious plan. That He would instill pieces of His own creative spirit in the likes of sinful people like me, like these people sitting all around me … it was almost too much to bear.

Never had I seen so many creative types in one place, and it was obvious something big was happening inside us all. To help us make sense of the collective "something big," the next session's speaker urged us to look back into our childhood and write down those few, key creative things we used to love to do. For me, the memories instantly came flooding back.

As far back as I can remember, nothing gave me greater joy as a kid than when a new box of crayons made their way into my hands. My favorite was the box that held sixty-four spectacular colors featuring the famous Built-In Sharpener on the back. Opening the lid, I would close my eyes and inhale the wonderful, waxy aroma. I truly believed each crayon had been handpicked and placed in this particular Crayola box just for me. Still do, actually.

Several "masterpieces" later, the bright yellow container that once held a rainbow of color looked more like the chew toy of a rabid dog. The paper wrappers were torn, and the once perfectly pointy tips were worn down to pathetic nubs. It was on such occasions that the pronouncement came, me to my mom: "A new box clearly must be purchased." It was the only time she took orders from me. She knew not to mess with the Crayola Cycle.

Coloring and I were close friends, but my *very* favorite thing to do as a kid was to put on backyard productions. I would enlist whomever was around—my sister, our cousins, friends who lived within walking distance and were willing to be my "stars" for the afternoon. We had two elaborate stages: the backyard swing set on days that were nice, and my parents' front porch when the rainstorms came.

I'd make tickets and promotional posters by hand and then

would hang blankets over the swing set to act as a grand curtain. The last of my preshow duties was to arrange the lawn chairs so that everyone was guaranteed a good seat.

Our shows always adhered to a winning format. We'd each do whatever tricks were in our arsenal at the present time—backflips, twirling routines, dance numbers—while saving the Special Song for the finale. After thunderous applause from our family members who'd so graciously agreed to show up one more time for one more amateur performance, I'd put everything away and immediately begin evaluating what we could do differently the next time around. It was the occupational hazard of a producer, which is the role I typically filled since it gave me license to be the bossy big cheese.

Every now and again, however, I'd make a special appearance as a performer and sing whatever happened to be my favorite song that particular week. Singing had always come naturally to me, and in grade school, nothing elated me more than weekly music class.

Every Thursday morning, Mrs. Seaford (or, "Mrs. Seafood," as my giggling nine-year-old friends and I deemed her) and her ever-present pitch pipe would arrive in our fourth-grade classroom promptly at ten o'clock for our weekly music session. And on good weeks, she'd instruct a handful of us to prepare a song to perform solo for the entire class.

The day came when it was to be my turn to go it alone, and in honor of the occasion I donned my special pink dress and pink, yellow, and lime-green toe socks. I asked my mom to pull my hair back with my favorite headband, and, to boost confidence even further, I wrote out my lyrics to Olivia Newton John's "I Honestly Love You" on a sheet of my purple notebook paper. Everyone knows you can't foul up when purple notebook paper is involved.

When Mrs. Seafood called my name, I reached for my lyric sheet with sweaty palms. I contorted my nervous face into a fake smile as I made my way to the front of the classroom and proceeded to belt out that song like I was on a Broadway stage.

Once I had finished singing and the applause from my classmates died down, I headed back to my seat. *Whew! I did it!* But before I could sit down, Mrs. Seafood had one of her Grand Ideas. "Now, Cynthia, it is quite obvious that you *know* those lyrics, so I would like for you to sing the whole song again, but this time without your notebook paper blocking your pretty little face."

I could have died. Or at least fainted. Right there on the grayish-brown all-purpose carpet of the Willard Elementary School fourth-grade classroom.

So, with my cheeks and neck on fire with embarrassment, I peered out over the top of my classmates' heads, found a focal point on the crooked map of the United States hanging on the back wall, and sang from my heart the words to a song I knew absolutely nothing about. That part didn't seem to matter, however, because once I had finished, Mrs. Seafood looked at me and with sincerity I'd previously never felt, said, "You have a lot to offer this world, Cynthia. *Now*, you may take your seat."

Who knows what her words were supposed to mean. I surely didn't at the time. But somehow, over the decades, memories of words like those have lingered in my mind. Somewhere along the way, words like "You have a lot to offer to this world, Cynthia" actually became something I believed.

DITCHING THE DREAM

"Become an artist" isn't something that typically appears on the What I Want to Be When I Grow Up top-ten list. It just doesn't seem to fit with society's demands that we all grow up, get married, and raise two-point-five perfect children. It stands to reason, then, that like so many artists I've talked to over the years, I stepped away from being "creative" immediately after graduating from high school. I ditched the "artist dream" for my *real* dream of becoming a homemaker, a wife, a mom. "June, Ward, Wally, and the Beave"—that was the vision I had for myself, despite what encouraging things youth pastors, teachers, and my own family members said. Though they tried valiantly to convince me otherwise, it just never registered in my brain that the creative things I'd so joyously engaged in as a kid could actually equate to God's design for my future.

Sure, the stresses of life can be overwhelming as years tick by and
obligations add up.
But every time "life" wins a victory—however small—
another canvas gets covered up and placed
in the back of the closet,
another brush gets laid down, another song goes unsung.

We point all of our energies toward taking care of family, taking care of work, taking care of the laundry, the bills, and the lawn, all the while neglecting to take care of our *yes*. What are the creative gifts you have been given? What are you doing to feed them and use them and let them breathe?

But who has time to chase creative dreams? They get chalked up to childish flights of fancy, and perhaps without even realizing it, we stick the invitation back on the shelf, telling ourselves that some time, someday, we'll accept it once more. It just can't be today.

This, I believe, is not the way God intended for it to be.

THE ORIGINAL CALLING FORTH

There is a story in the book of Exodus that wrecks the part of me that's willing to ditch the artist dream every time I read it. It's the story of God giving Moses instructions for exactly how He wanted the tabernacle built.

Moses had just spent forty solid days in the presence of God. Coming off of that rather long meeting with a yellow legal pad full of reminders in hand, Moses gathered all of the Israelites together and started to tick things off his list. First up was getting the work/rest balance right.

"Well, so, you've heard that we've got this tabernacle to build," I envision him saying to the captive audience standing before him. "For starters, I need to tell you that each and every week, we're going to work six days straight and then take one off. That seventh one is a 'holy day' and the penalty for bending the rules here is pretty stiff, so just go with me on this."

Moses proceeded to lay out every ounce of detail God had provided, including what materials to use, what measurements had to be met, what furniture needed to be built, and the precise procedures the whole team was to follow. There was a whole slew of artists in the crowd that day, so I imagine Moses lost at least

a portion of his audience during his endless litany of specifica-
tions, instructions, deadlines, and regulations. Somewhere in his
discourse, though, the people must have recognized a strange, spiritual anointing on this particular project, because the text explains
that after Moses dismissed his meeting, the people rushed home,
garnered their resources, and returned to offer "freewill offerings
for all the work the LORD through Moses had commanded them to
do" (Ex. 35:29).

Moses knew that a compelling vision didn't mean diddly-
squat without willing souls who were ready to make it a reality.
As he looked into the eyes of the men and women standing before
him—unexpected artists whose arms clutched priceless fabrics and
ornate jewelry and dyed yarn and hides of sea cows, of all things—
he realized God had provided some creative collaboration for him
after all.

Two of the collaborators went by the names Bezalel and Oholiab,
and these guys had some pretty interesting things going for them. First
and foremost, they were filled with the Spirit of God. But in addition
to that, they had already been equipped with "skill, ability and knowledge in all kinds of crafts—to make artistic designs for work in gold,
silver and bronze, to cut and set stones, to work in wood and to engage
in all kinds of artistic craftsmanship" (Ex. 35:31–33).

So here we have it, the first two artists
being "called forth."
Everything they needed for the creative,
God-given task at hand
had already been placed right inside of them.

It's impossible to know for sure what was going through their minds as they learned of this monumental thing they were called to create. I mean, a *tabernacle*? Where God was going to hang out? Pretty heavy stuff. But knowing they were artists through and through, I have to wonder if, rather than pondering the massive implications of fumbling the task, they were challenging each of Moses' commands instead. "Scarlet, purple, and blue? You think you're going to establish an engaging and worshipful vibe with *that* color palette?"

I'm sure that when they saw the blueprints, they fought to extend the length of the building for better feng shui. When they were told they had to use fifty bronze clasps to secure the tent covering, I just bet they asked why they couldn't they get by with thirty. You know, free up a few budget dollars for a new soundboard or more candles instead.

Whatever their ponderings and push-backs, though, one thing is certain: At some point along the way, they said yes. God Himself had called them forth by name, issuing their personalized invitations through His good buddy Moses. And their creative contribution— nothing less than the dwelling place of God—would affect all of Christendom.

Granted, Bezalel and Oholiab could have hung back in the crowd or come late to the meeting or said no outright, but the text reads they tirelessly and faithfully worked, made, cast, and overlaid to create a home for the almighty God.

ME, AN ARTIST?

I met with some artist friends lately, and eventually, the conversation meandered to the discussion of when each of us knew we were creative. We were trying to probe those original sparks that first told us we were artists. Rita, an incredible oil painter, said she could remember being creative even at the age of two. Her father, an artist as well, evidently encouraged her to follow her artistic bloodline the day she emerged from the womb.

cre·a·tive [krE-'A-tiv], adjective
1 : marked by the ability or power to create : given to creating <the creative impulse>
2 : having the quality of something created rather than imitated

What is the earliest "creative" thing you can remember doing?
Do you consider yourself "creative"?
How do you feel when someone refers to you as "creative"?

Another friend named Orlen was given acrylic paints as a gift at forty. His first painting was of a young woman sitting beside a table of flowers. Without a model or a photograph before him, he painted from his mind's eye alone. Orlen thought that *maybe* he might be creative, but it wasn't until his early sixties that he embraced the idea of being an artist.

Waiting—Orlen Weaver

Terry grew up with a mother who was a painter, but interestingly, she was never encouraged to paint as a child. For her, it wasn't until she was out of college that the realization hit. She was an artist after all.

What about me—was *I* an artist? I didn't own six hundred tubes of paint. I didn't have "pieces" hanging in a gallery. I wasn't making a living selling art at shows.

Since I didn't fit my own framework for who an artist was, I began to wonder if perhaps God had delivered my invitation to the wrong address. But in my heart of hearts, I knew better. Despite all my failings and flaws, God was requesting *my* presence. "I formed you and fashioned you and gifted you for this," He was saying. "You are *My* artist, and I think you're terrific. The choice is yours, but you should know that I definitely choose you! I pick *you* to come create with Me and for Me … for My glory."

art·ist [ˈär-tist], noun
1 : one skilled or versed in learned arts
2 : one who professes and practices an imaginative art
3 : a skilled performer
4 : one who is adept at something

What is your definition of "artist"?
What assumptions, experiences, and input throughout
your life helped to form that definition?
Do you meet the requirements of your own definition?

Who along the way has influenced
your artistic tendencies?

Author Anne Lamott wrote about a Sunday-morning ritual she engages in with the kids she teaches in her Sunday-school class. It's called Loved and Chosen, and the basic gist is that she plops down on the classroom couch and looks carefully at the mass of children in front of her. Observing what each of them is wearing, she begins the game. In *Grace (Eventually)*, she describes a typical occurrence this way:

> I sat on the couch and glanced slowly around in a goofy, menacing way, and then said, "Is anyone here wearing a blue sweater with Pokémon on it?" The four-year-old looked down at his chest, astonished to discover that he matched this description—like, What are the odds? "Come over here to the couch," I said. "You are so loved and so chosen." He clutched at himself like a beauty pageant finalist.[1]

The magic of the game is that Lamott continues on this way until every last child has been told that he or she is indeed *so* loved and *so* chosen.

When my "invitation" had arrived, somewhere from deep down inside of me, I knew I, too, was being invited to a different sort of couch and told that I was loved and chosen. Using everything from my childhood love of crayons and backyard productions to my passion for photography, music, and video, God had a plan to use it all and bring glory to Himself.

The truth was, I *wanted* to be chosen. And finally, once and for all, I knew that I had been. I wasn't crazy. I wasn't weird. There really was a place for me to belong. Sitting very still in that conference auditorium that afternoon, I bowed my softened heart and said, "God, I am Your artist. Use me however You see fit. I love You. Lead me down this new path to bring Your beauty to life and Your truth to people's lives. I hereby mark my RSVP card *yes*."

RE-UPPING YOUR YES

On a sunny Saturday morning in March last year, a group of ladies and I met to explore the possibility of their starting a visual-arts group in their church in Wyoming. Donna, Jill, and Kathy had once held a passion for painting, but upon the arrival of children, little league, and the PTA, they had neither the time nor the energy to create.

Once their kids were grown and finally out of the house, these three "former artists" wondered if their creative potential still existed, or if it had somehow evaporated over time. They sat across from me asking question after question about living life from their creative side, when finally it dawned on me: What they were really requesting was permission—they wanted *an invitation to create*.

With just a few words of encouragement and their own belief that maybe, just maybe, they could start again—sort of "re-up their yes"—they headed to a local art shop and filled their shopping baskets with brushes, canvases, and dozens of tubes of paint.

Months later, one of the ladies contacted me and shared that she'd taken my advice and had recently sold her first painting.

Twenty years after the canvas had
disappeared into the closet,
this mother, wife, cook, veritable taxi driver, and friend
reclaimed her status as artist.
She discovered her spark of passion for painting
was not only still there,
but that it had welled up into a raging fire.

I heard this news and immediately thought of Paul's encouragement to Timothy to "fan into flame the gift of God," so that everyone watching would see His power and might (2 Tim. 1:6). When we give artists permission to resume being artists, *mighty* flames in our midst get fanned.

WHEN WHISPERS BELLOW

Several years before Pope John Paul departed this earth, he issued a letter to artists.

With this letter, I turn to you, the artists of the world, to assure you of my esteem and to help consolidate a more constructive partnership between art and the Church. Mine is an invitation to rediscover the depth of the spiritual and religious dimension that has been typical of art in its noblest forms in every age. It is with this in mind that I appeal to you, artists of the written and spoken word, of the theater and music, of the plastic arts and the most recent technologies in the field of communication.

I appeal especially to you, Christian artists: I wish to remind each of you that, beyond functional considerations,

the close alliance that has always existed between the gospel
and art means that you are invited to use your creative intu-
ition to enter into the heart of the mystery of the Incarnate
God and at the same time into the mystery of humanity.[2]

What an invitation! Oh, how I wish I had known so many years ago that it had been extended to me. To be sure, I've had a few cheerleaders along the way. But what I would have given for one of them to sit me down early on, look me dead in the eye, and say, "Cindy, what are you doing with your life and the creative gifts you've been given? Do you understand that, to whom much is given, much is required?" (Luke 12:48 NLT). Would I have even listened? What's more, would I have known how to respond?

My pride and easily distracted personality admits a "probably not" on both counts. To think about the mistakes I could have avoided along the way, the impact on more lives I could have known, the wasted moments of ego-driven creativity I could have *not* known … oh, man.

I shudder to think in those terms. (So I think I'll move on.)

The same God who created "in the beginning," who in spoken words caused the entire galaxy to be birthed from nothing, who wove color into light from darkness, who placed within us His own creativity—*this* God has never once given up on me, all along the point-A-to-point-B path. He has continued to find different ways—sometimes using insightful friends, different art forms, even nature itself—to speak in whispers that have bellowed for my attention to know there is a *continual* invitation for me to collaborate with Him.

And for you to do the same.

Your presence is requested.
And it's never too late to show up.

My artist-friend Orlen didn't start painting until he was in his forties. Over the last seven years, he's taken classes, sought feedback, and learned new techniques. At a recent Art Guild show, Orlen—now sixty-seven—submitted two entries and received his first ribbon on a piece that demonstrated a brand-new technique he was testing. "Aren't you glad there's no age limit on when we can begin creating?" I asked him.

He just grinned.

My Wyoming artist-friends didn't reclaim their creative ground until they were empty-nesters.

And then there was Moses. The guy didn't even *open* his invitation until the ripe old age of eighty. When you say yes, you open yourself up to inspired creativity that is born in the very heart of God. If the only thing that's required of you is simply to show up, then you must know that He already has the creative ideas and the painstaking details worked out. Ephesians 2:10 (MSG) says it this way: "He creates each of us by Christ Jesus to join him in the work he does, the good work he has *gotten ready* for us to do, work we had better be doing."

The works are ready. But you have to show up. You first have to say yes. And just as was the case for Bezalel and Oholiab, you already hold the invitation in your hands. As you dive into coming chapters, I pray you see for yourself that the One who knows everything about you—the good, the bad, the ugly—is waiting to see if your response to His invitation into a marvelous, mind-blowing, unmerited, creative collaboration with the original Creator will indeed be *yes*.

One more thought, as it relates to the artist's yes: The "yes before the yes" for the artist is the "yes" of life-submission to the Creator Himself. I wonder if you have made the decision to surrender your life—and your art—to God. A simple prayer and a sincere heart—that's all it takes.

God, I acknowledge that Your Son, Jesus Christ, came to earth as a man in order to live a sinless life—the life I can't live, no matter how hard I try. He died in my place so that I don't have to die an eternal death. He paid the penalty I owe for my sin so that I don't have to pay it, and right here, right now, I want to accept that payment. I confess my past life of sin to You, I confess my desire to live for myself and to obey my own cravings instead of obeying You. I admit that I am now ready to trust Jesus as my Lord. I ask You into my heart—into my life—today. Please take up residence there and make me a new person, a new artist, for Your glory. I pray these things, believing that Jesus is my King, Amen.

As an artist—a "creative type"—how does your
art manifest itself today?
What are the monumental points along the way that have
grown you up from crayons to backyard productions
to where you are now? Write out your response—or
sketch it, draw it, paint it, sing it—remembering that
every step along the way is a very critical step.

-3-
WHEN ART WAS GOD'S ALONE

Life Outside the Invitation

In the beginning …
—THE CREATION ACCOUNT, THE BOOK OF GENESIS

ART IS PRETTY much my life. I speak about it, I write about it, I create it, I enjoy it in ways that shouldn't even be legal. My home displays it—both inside and out. My drive to work is captivated by it. And all day, every day, I'm enveloped by it in an office decorated to be nine-tenths art museum with just a smidge of productive workspace thrown in for good measure.

My job requires my attendance in at least two left-brain meetings a week, and in that context, this rather passionate love affair with art I've got going presents more than its share of challenges. I try to stay focused on the wildly stimulating topics of conversation that tend to unfold—budget line items and strategic-plan progress and attendance trends—but the *artiste* in me always responds the same way. I find the color of the spreadsheet's columns immensely more intriguing than the numbers themselves; I pay closer attention to the fonts on the report than to the words of the strategy summary I'm supposed to be reading; and I happen to think our most productive meetings to date have been the ones where I was allowed to issue a ban on all things fluorescent and introduce the glow of candles and soft, indirect lighting instead.

Sometimes there is even complete darkness. Every once in a while, a coworker shows up, prepared to deliver his or her ministry update using a laptop and a projector. And every time, I get all abuzz with excitement—*Wahoo! We get a show!*—until the PowerPoint title slide comes into focus, one-dimensional blue with bold, white, Times New Roman statistics and nary an interesting graphic to be found. Argh!

During one such presentation recently, I sort of let my mind wander to a new creative endeavor I had been working on, and a few minutes after I'd zoned out, a colleague leaned over and whispered, "Cindy, you're humming out loud. I can hear you from over here."

I said I was sorry and offered a sheepish grin, but it was no use. The sum of the senior leadership team has come to expect such accidental antics from their resident hummer/singer/painter/photographer. Creativity is in my blood. When you get me, you get creativity—this is something they have all come to tolerate. And, secretly, maybe even enjoy.

But I must confess, there are stretches of time when "being creative" comes so naturally that I find myself taking for granted my skills or talent or ability. I start to view my imagination and artistic competency as my right, rather than as the God-given birthright it actually is.

This "artistic entitlement" is a danger zone, and recently, I discovered I'm not alone in my proneness to tumble toward it.

ARTISTIC RIGHT OR PRIVILEGE?

I had a one-on-one chat recently with one of our church's visual artists. The conversation was lighthearted and enjoyable until she spoke up with a troubling observation. "Cindy, I think some of our artists are beginning to take our gallery for granted," she said. "They seem to have forgotten the day when our church walls were blank, the visual-arts community didn't exist, and all of us painters and sculptors and graphic designers were relegated to picking and choosing community art shows to enter instead of having a safe place where we could display our art—any form, any style, and in any manner that was prompted by God. It seems to me they think they're entitled to all of this."

The gallery she was referring to had been the brainchild of our visual-arts community during our very first meeting. We thought that the bare walls of our church's sanctuary demanded something artsy, and there was a lot of initial energy to take care of that ourselves. While I couldn't *factually* confirm or refute her assessment, I had to agree that the artists' interest in the gallery shows did seem to be waning a bit.

I began the very next visual-arts meeting by posing a simple question to the group sitting before me: "What would you say if I told you that the photography show that was hung just last week would be our last—that unfortunately, we were being forced to close down our gallery?"

Gasps of horror. It's the only way I can describe the group's reaction. Half the air was sucked right out of the room as collectively their posture rose to attention. And then came the questions.

"But where will we go to display our work?"

"What do you mean shut it down? I *need* it! It's the only catalyst I have to stretch me in my art!"

"Who made *that* decision? The congregation would miss it. In fact, *they* need it as much as *we* do!"

"It's not just the congregation but the *community* that would miss it! After all the great shows, the hard work … now you're taking it *away*?"

The pace of the questioning made the questions themselves seem rhetorical. But finally, an artist looked me straight in the eye and slowly said four words I had no choice but to respond to: "Is this for real?"

I let the question hang in the air for a few seconds. And during those seconds, I realized that if I didn't divulge the honest truth, I could very well face a good, old-fashioned, first-century stoning. By Christian artists, no less. It wouldn't be pretty, and so I confessed the reality of our situation. "It is, in fact … not for real.

"But in the same breath, can I ask you a few questions?" I continued. "What if it *were* for real? What if I told you that this church, which has freed you up as artists to explore your creativity and cultivate it and let it manifest itself in all sorts of ways—including that of having a hallway gallery—what if I told you that the support and structure and artistic playground you have found here really *were* to go away?

"I guess the question behind the question is this," I said. "Do you ever take your art—your creativity, the abilities you have, the opportunities this church gives us—do you ever catch yourself possibly taking it all for *granted?*"

I waited in silence until, one by one, they began to share thoughts on their respective creative journeys and what it means for them to be an active artist, a contributing artist, a *valued* artist—let alone, in the context of a thriving local church. Most had never dreamed they would be a part of something so special.

> I didn't intend to wreck my artists' day; I simply wanted to
> send a clear and compelling message: The extraordinary
> gift of being able to create—to bring ideas and inspirations
> to life—must never be taken for granted.

Art wasn't always our privilege. Creating wasn't always ours to do. There wasn't always an invitation sitting in our mailboxes. There was, in fact, a time when only God created, a time when the only artist community in existence was comprised of three members—Father, Son, and Holy Spirit. There was a time when art was God's alone.

CREATIVITY'S BIRTHPLACE

The time had come. The moment was now, an eternally anticipated moment for God—the one, true, divine Artist. Inside of the only "uncreated" imagination history would ever know, color, shape, and texture fashioned themselves into images longing to be united, desperate to exist.

All that Artist had dreamed would soon come to life. He had taken pains to imagine each and every detail—largest to the oh, so small—inside, outside each creative endeavor that was about to be flung into formation.

The Very Grand Plan about to be executed would never be

matched by another. Much would be required of Artist during the process, but His commitment to the work was far higher than any price to be paid. When the canvas was finally finished, blank no more, there would be no finer work of art available and, consequently, no greater celebration known.

With His strength and power and words as His at-the-ready paintbrushes, Artist released that which to that point had been held captive by His mind. Eyeing the vast, dark canvas below, He saw limitless possibilities.

Artist felt the rush of excitement well up,
His heart thumping faster and faster,
His breath quickening,
as without any hesitation,
He voiced creation into existence,
the heavens and the earth now being beckoned to life.

The earth—even more glorious, more stunning in the real than in the imagined—stopped short His breath. Artist hovered over the surface of the deep, looked upon the earth, and knew much would be needed to prepare it for what was to come. *Shape. This is the moment's missing ingredient.* Earth hung suspended in the darkness, void of form, anxiously awaiting context and boundary lines and a clean silhouette. Its raw and ragged and ill-defined state would never support all that Artist had in store for it to hold. And so He continued, creating accordingly to the Very Grand Plan.

With a gentle whisper that may at once have sounded as strong as peeling thunder, "Let there be light."

At once, darkness danced with light, intermingling, swirling, invading one another. They played like schoolchildren, light chasing darkness until she caught up, then coyly turning, darting away. Artist laughed a hearty laugh and further separated the two. He knew this was good. The light will be "day," the darkness, "night," He declared. The first morning and first evening. A smile, a nod, an agreement with Himself that all was going according to plan—the Very Grand Plan. And yet this was only the beginning.

Days two and three. Artist continued creating, His steady rhythm of idea-meets-implementation, concept-reaches-execution. Separating the water into two layers—one upper, titled sky, and one lower in place called the sea. The dry ground wound its way from beneath the water and appeared to Artist, requesting its name. "Land," it would be called.

Then a pause, a look, more of a canvas coming to life. He liked what He saw, for it was … it was *good*.

Each day Artist upped the ante on His inventiveness. He had taken three days to give the earth shape. Now, *forming* would give way to *filling*. Land, created just yesterday, had embarked on its own creative process, producing seed-bearing plants, trees, and vegetation. Artist had toyed with several colors before landing on green, which seemed to suit them well. He now admired His handiwork as it glowed against the bright, vivid sapphire sky. Closing His eyes, He reflected on color as He had first dreamed it up. Nearly intoxicating, those magentas and periwinkles and emeralds and mauves. All that had been created thus far seemed to puff out its chest, proud of its vibrancy and nuance and depth. Color—living, breathing, moving, pulsating color. It was good. It was right. And once again, Artist smiled.

With an authoritative tone, Artist spoke into existence two great lights, which would function as guides for the turning of the days, the nights, the seasons. He marveled at their power, their clarity, their magnetic personalities as the rest of the solar system systematically marched 'round and 'round, casting shadows on land and sea. Entranced, He reached out long fingers to touch the sun, then cooled their tips with a dip in the sea.

With low whispers He called each star by name, watching with great delight as they played cosmic hide-and-seek, rushing this way and that, shushing those crouched nearby so as not to be found. Then, quietly and gently, as only a father can, Artist directed them to assigned places.

Awe and wonder and amazement filling their lungs, the entire universe sang in unison, worshipping their Creator. Oh, how they agreed this was all a Very Grand Plan.

Artist paused to listen, His heart warming to the lovely strains.

Day five dawned, and Artist couldn't wait to get started. Creatures would be the priority, a welcome release for Artist's imagination, which was chock-full of spots and stripes and fur. *On the land and the sea. Yes, I will put them everywhere!*

His laughter rolled through the heavens as He watched from His studio. Each creature spoken into existence, quite startled at first, shook out its body, cleared its focus, cocked its head in curiosity—*What am I? Who am I? Where did I come from?*

Water-bound models tested fins and feet and breathing apparatus, anxious to know if they would sink or stay afloat, while the ones on land walked and ran in fits and starts, pushing legs to their limit with flips and jumps and splits. Winged creatures soared in the sky, giving grace to the clouds and presence to the air.

Large and small, He had created every one. *How pleasing these creatures are to Me!* He thought. *I must tell them so.* Continuing to admire His handiwork, He called them all together and blessed them by declaring that there should be more of them: "Be fruitful and multiply!" came the divine instruction.

Each created being bowed just as the cosmos itself had done days before, in worship to the One who had given it life.

Artist looked at His canvas, taking note of everything in its proper place, except that which would be His finest masterpiece. For now, a blank spot dead-center interrupted the flow of beautiful formation, but soon—very soon—the middle of Artist's canvas would be occupied by the crown of all creation.

Artist stirred the dust of the ground with the warmth of His breath until suddenly, stunningly, spiritually, a torso emerged. A head, a face, two eyes, two ears, a nose, a mouth, two arms, two legs.

The work of art lay perfectly still,
ever so quiet, ever so brilliant.

Spectacular!

The triune Artist shared a sigh of astonishment. *Man! We have created … man.*

Artist peered inside this ultimate creation and patiently, confidently confirmed His design. Two-hundred and six bones. Ribs. Liver. Veins. Brain. Emotions. Creativity. And then, there was the heart—the most magnificent of centerpieces. He had shaped it after His own and secured deep within it a seat of longing—an insatiable craving, expanding over time, satisfied only by relating with Him. *What joy My companionship will bring this creature!* He reasoned. *I have known him as no other ever will. I will love him better than he imagines himself lovable. As of this moment, we will be one. That is My heart's desire.*

All was as it should be, and Artist bent low, placing His mouth over man's mouth, breathing gentle, passionate puffs of life into man's lungs until at once, fingers and toes wiggled and writhed, eyes jittered under lids, nose twitched and sneezed and with that … the first exhale of human life.

The man coughed and sputtered and pulled himself up to his right-side elbow, looking all around to get his bearings, mentally reaching for the sense of it all. He came to his knees, determined to rise, to move, to go somewhere, but his immediacy was stilled by the presence of God.

Artist looked full-faced toward His masterpiece,
and the art could only remain facedown.

As the stars, the trees, the creatures, and cosmos had done, man praised Artist with an overflowing heart. "I will worship You all of my days!" he exclaimed. "As of this moment, we will be one. I know no deeper desire!"

Artist slowly swirled around the man, watching, admiring, nodding His head in soulish approval, and with the slight tug upward of His mouth, grinned a wider grin than He knew He could grin.

The following day, Artist stepped down into His canvas to show the man around. "Here is what I have been doing this week," He beamed.

The man was elated. "All for me?" he asked.

"All for you, to care for and to enjoy," came Artist's reply.

Everything He had created—the garden, with lively hues and budding aromas, and fruit you could peel back with your own bare hand. When He sensed man was ready, Artist sat him down to share with him their first collaboration. "We will name the creatures," Artist explained. "I have built them, fashioned them, decorated them, but I saved the best part for last. It is your part—to decide what they shall be called. You will give them their *identity.*"

Artist requested the presence of those that roamed, those that frolicked in the sea; today would be their big day. The procession flowed forth, man's wide eyes taking them in one by one, each distinct from all others. Artist nodded at man's logical designations of pointer and grasshopper and tree frog, suppressing chuckles at the likes of "hippopotamus" and "yellow-bellied platypus."

How beautifully everything had come together! This, from careful planning and a thorough design. And now, all of creation held its breath as they awaited evaluation. They strained to hear what their Artist would say. "Good. This is good. In fact, it's *very* good indeed."

At the sound of those words, the universe broke into wild waves of applause. Their loving Creator had accomplished His goal. And now, it was His time to pause.

In six smart days, the vast canvas had adopted color, lived out light, taken on texture, and birthed living, breathing beings. Artist wasn't so much wearied as desirous of rest—preventive, decisive, appropriate rest. He stepped back from His creation and reflected on all that He had made. What was initiated by His imagination now existed in the realm of what's real. *Yes, a Very Grand Plan.*

Artist had known it would not be good for man to live alone, and so at one moment, He allowed man to fall into a deep sleep. He took one of man's ribs and carefully, meticulously formed another living being. Man would have a helper, a mate whom he would call *woman.*

Artist, man, and woman related to one another in the precise way Artist had planned, walking and talking and laughing together, enjoying the others' company as they experienced their garden paradise. Truly, they possessed every good thing. Their shared love, their devotion, their commitment was unabashed, pure, perfect, and free.

But then, in one devastating moment, darkness caught light and smothered the colors on the canvas by way of a fateful choice.

The tempting tree.

The crafty serpent.

The clever lie.

The choice of disobedience.

The very

> first

> > sin.

All that was perfect, marred. All that was right, made wrong. All that was free, now bound.

Bleakness,

> darkness,

> > coldness,

> > > ruin.

Artist knew that it must come to this, despite a miniscule seed of hope He held that perhaps the right choice would be made, His stern warnings obeyed. But now, as He eyed the canvas, it seemed He held only His grief.

I must banish them from the garden. The thought rolled through His mind but struggled to find a sticking place. *My living, breathing works of art have chosen against Me. They have chosen a deeper desire other than oneness with Me.*

Over time, Artist observed the extent of man's wickedness on the earth and saw that everything man and woman thought and imagined—the very imagination He Himself had given them—was stained with evil throughout. He regretted their presence, their formation, their sin.

He wept bitter tears that spilled over from an all-too-bruised heart. Artist knew He must destroy His art. Oh, but this was not how it was to be—dashed dreams and unfulfilled expectations, a once-flawless canvas now marred to the point of deserving destruction. Or requiring redemption.

But Artist's original longing never waned but instead only grew. He had foreseen this terrible challenge and so, reflexively, He unfurled a new paintbrush and created new colors—costly colors that would paint into existence a glorious hue of redemption. *More time, more ingenuity, more patience, more elaborate detail, and, yes, more cost*—He compassionately calculated the eternal price He would pay. *I will devote Myself to repairing My art, and eventually it will bring Me even greater pleasure.*

From His studio high above the canvas, Artist continued creating until it was complete.

As you read Genesis chapters 1 and 2, what do you see?
What do you hear?
Taste?
Feel?

What role is God playing in the scene you experience?
How does it compare or contrast to the
one articulated in this chapter?

Do you enjoy the "creation scene" of your own artwork?
Which projects have been "very good"?

Stop and give God thanks. And then linger with the
creative process ... the planning and the dreaming
and the seeing of it. Let it astound you in its
intricacy and move you with its complexity.

ONENESS WITH GOD, OUR DEEPEST DESIRE

Last summer I was heading eastward across the Colorado state line,
en route to my folks' house in Missouri. The trip out was always
a perfect time to decompress. Blaring tunes, the cool wind in my
hair, a cell phone in the "off" position—I wanted nothing more
than to make good time and to release every care in the world. As
I careened down the highway, I heard a silent but all-too-audible
voice say, *Watch.*

I turned down the radio, listened more closely, and still, all I
could hear was the whir of rubber tires on asphalt and my golden
retriever Bo's panted snoring from the back of the SUV.

Watch.

There it was again. *Who's talking to me?*

I looked in my rearview mirror, I looked at the empty passenger
seat, and I turned around and stared at Bo. Nothing. If this was some
sort of prompting from God, then what in the world was I supposed
to be watching? It was barely six in the morning. The only watchable
thing I could see were headlights heading toward me four lanes over.

Having no idea what it all meant, I put down my coffee cup, relaxed my spine into the seat, positioned my hands at ten and two, exhaled with a deep sigh, and focused on all that was whizzing by as I did seventy-five down the road.

Which all happened, as it turned out, just in time for the start of the show.

Though the sun could not yet be seen, the black sky before me became an incredible mixture of midnight blue and bright emerald green, a hint of turquoise tossed in for fun. As if fast-forwarding my morning, God introduced gold, then orange, then red within moments of having my attention.

"How do You do that?" I asked. Bo suddenly sat up, his ears rising in anticipation.

Minutes later, the sun heralded the dawn of yet another day, hugging the vast horizon with arms outstretched. *Good morning!* my thoughts responded as light flooded the world around me. God went on this way, ushering in newness and color and all things good, from start to finish, a show that lasted a hundred and eighteen minutes, by my count. And quite a show it was! Not to mention quite a way to start my trip. Driving through the state of Kansas had never been such a spiritual experience, but today, as I dabbed the corners of my eyes with my sleeve, I knew I had opened a gift straight from God.

I stopped at Starbucks—which is *always* a spiritual experience— and stretched all six of Bo's and my legs before making our way back to the interstate. Poofs of cumulous cotton somersaulted across the sky, rolling and colliding with themselves, the sun's light now relegated to slight beams that burst forth when the clouds weren't looking.

The result was a series of spectacular spotlights that made shades of green pop on nearby rolling hills. Tiny raindrops began to splat on my windshield that became fat drops that became an outright downpour. I finally conceded the victory to the skies and threw on my wipers.

Heavy rain, rays of sunshine, gray clouds giving way to white, sullen sky shining bright, bright blue.

"In the beginning" wasn't just a onetime thing, I thought, now understanding why God was asking me to watch. It's still happening today. God is still creating. Artist is making something new, allowing light to chase away darkness, inviting me to dance in colorful, meaningful, vital collaboration with Him. Daily I am being asked, "Will you participate in My glorious creativity?"

Hours later, I pulled into my parents' driveway, thoroughly exhausted and yet more alive than I had been in a long, long time. As I lifted the hatch and watched Bo bound toward the front door, I resolved in my heart never to take my art—my creativity and inspiration and competency—for granted again. *Oneness with You, God … I know no deeper desire*—those are the syllables that beat through my heart as I moved from the truck to the house.

Artist could have withheld His wonderful gift of creativity from me.
And yet He did not.
He could have kept it all to Himself.
And yet He did not.

In the gift of art—collaborative art that leans into Him and leverages us—our pain is soothed, our groaning eased as we wait for the promise of One's coming return; He is restoring the canvas to its original intent. In that moment, Artist, who once held everything … everything in His imagination, will again stand back, He will grin a wide grin, and He will whisper, "This is very, very good."[1]

-part 2-

HEART TO HEART

~4~
CHOOSING SOUL
Obedience Afoot in the Artistic Life

4 August 1998

The jar is plain—simple lines, a light terra-cotta color, the surface rough with uneven nicks and deep scratches. It stands twelve inches high with handles that swirl down from either side of the neck. You can actually see prints at the base of those handles, right where artist thumbs pushed and smooshed them into the body of the jar.

Old Colorado City, after two months of searching for just the right one. The others were way too shiny, too polished. But without really knowing what I was looking for, the hunt went on. Process of elimination paid off.

Monday afternoon, I wandered into that pottery shop at 30th Street and Cimarron—the one with the outdoor patio around back. Super-tall shelving unit, and there on the bottom row sat my jar. It had been exposed to the elements for who knows how long, sun and rain and hail and snow so common here. I kind of liked that about it. It had weathered a lot, and yet it still stood strong, steady … all by itself. In an instant, I knew this was the one.

NEARLY A DECADE ago, I wrote those words in my journal. It was exactly the fourth day of August, and I was exactly a mess. I had awakened one morning seven weeks prior to that day with a crystal-clear image imprinted in my mind. It was of five black-and-white photographs of a broken jar that somehow gets all put back together as the scene progresses. The background was black with a single source of light coming from the upper-right-hand corner. There was a white mat around the lot of them, the entire piece framed in thick black and gray marble.

In a matter of seconds, the image was burned into my sleepy, hot-tea-craving consciousness. There was no escaping it. I woke up with it. I drove to work with it. I led two meetings with it. Evidently, I was supposed to create it. And so finally, I sat down with it in my office and sketched it out on a piece of paper. Undeniably, there was an urgency—a "drivenness"—to get this particular piece of art created.

REFLECTION: SPIRAL STAIRCASE DOWNWARD

4 August 1998 (continued)

Mark and Brenda surprised me today with a makeshift studio they had crafted in the basement of their home. I made the mistake of telling them about the jar project; the studio was a practical place to get my work done without being rushed or distracted or interrupted, but I think it was also their not-so-subtle way of saying, "We're not letting you off the hook,

Cindy. If we have anything to say about it, this is going to get done."

Before I could begin the photography part, the jar needed to be crushed. My plan was to break it into pieces, glue it back together, and then photograph it in reverse order, removing one piece at a time until the pieces formed a pile. Once I had the actual photographs, I would line them up in the right order to show, step by step, the jar finding its much needed restoration.

I sketched pencil lines where I thought the cracks should go and then with a chisel and hammer tap, tap, tapped along the lines. Pretty interesting how some of the cracks ran intuitively along the pencil marks I had drawn while others split off and went their own way. Certain areas—all along the jar's belly—were thick and more difficult to crack; even more pressure had to be applied.

This is just like you, Cindy, the thought occurred to me,
stubborn, independent, trying to follow your own way.
But I know the real you ...

A slight panic settled into my chest, but before God could go any further, I turned my attention back to my chiseling.

The path I was about to walk would wind down like a rickety and too-steep spiral staircase that plunged deeper and deeper and deeper, until God and I had passed the plastic surface of who I was pretending to be and carved our way into the core of what was hidden down below.

How far will you go to engage with this piece of art? The upsetting question could have just as easily come from the undercooked chicken I'd had for lunch as from the God of the universe Himself, but one thing was clear: Something was calling me to be present in a unique and powerful way.

Surface, or soul?

I remember making the decision right then, right there, that I'd at least attempt to be "real" with this project. As much as I was able, I'd create from my soul. Unfortunately, I wildly underestimated what that would require.

19 August 1998

A thin layer of dust covered the entire studio, and I was only making matters worse as my chisel kicked up puffs of progress all around me. I held still for a minute and looked at the pieces that once constituted a lovely jar. They were just a heap of rubble now, but it was precious rubble.

I started picking through the pile, gathering together

the larger pieces in the palm of my hand. It didn't take long to locate the ones that would re-form the base. I grabbed the hot-glue gun and with Mark's help, affixed pieces one at a time. Over and over, I painted a stripe of warm glue, rotated the piece into place, and carefully held it until it was ready to stay upright on its own.

Before we glued the final pieces in place, I stuffed a corded light bulb down into the bottom. The last photograph was supposed to be illuminated from within, if my dreamland vision was accurate. It was exciting to accomplish so much in a short period of time ... all I could think about was snapping the shots, jumping in my truck, and heading to the development lab—efficiency at its finest.

I used infrared film and had already loaded it into the camera. Brenda flicked the light switch off and turned on the jar-light. It was beautiful! Bright white beams burst through even the tiniest crack. Exactly what I had imagined that early morning in June.

Then … well, disaster.

The camera had only fired off three or four shots when something of a shotgun fired back. The jar exploded. I mean *exploded*. No idea what happened, but I'm guessing the heat from the bulb weakened the glue. For the second time that day, I found myself looking down on a chaotic heap of pottery pieces.

It was sort of funny at first—or maybe just shocking. But then a heavy silence hung in the air as I stood there, sizing up the mess. Mark and Brenda were speechless. As was I. My heartbeat throbbed inside my ears, a low, numbing thump pounding out a rhythm to God's still, small words: "Cindy, you are not going any further until you pay attention to what I'm asking you to pay attention to."

> I was a kid caught with her hand in the cookie jar.
> My arm was stuck, the world was spinning,
> my head was feverish,
> and I had no one to blame but myself.

My mind started to race. This is not about some nice,

little art project. This has nothing to do with a stupid
jar. This is about me.

I'd been running for so long, hiding, convincing myself
that I had it all together, that I was okay, really, I was.

Inside, I began to fall apart.

During my growing-up years, I loved to receive praise. More than
anything, I wanted to be a good girl because the better I was at being
good, the more praise I received. I was never very good at math, but
that equation was plain to see.

I wasn't perfect, to be sure. I made as many bad decisions as I did
good, I could be tremendously moody, and I was never once on the
honor roll, (although I always seemed to land an A in art class). But
still, I presented a perfect-enough façade so as to garner acceptance
and love from anyone and everyone in my midst: God, my parents,
my friends, my teachers ... and later from abusive boyfriends, angry
colleagues, and insecure bosses.

I swallowed my true feelings in favor of submission to everyone
else's expectations of what I would do or think or say or become.
My name was Steady, and my chief aim in life was to avoid rocking
the boat. If a friend asked what movie we should see, I'd say, "What
do *you* want to see?" If a coworker asked where we should go for
lunch, I'd say, "I don't care ... *you* pick." If my date asked my opinion
on anything, I'd poll him first and then go along with whatever he

thought would be best. I wasn't too far off Julia Roberts's character in the movie *Runaway Bride*, who didn't even know what type of eggs she liked. She had honestly never taken the time to find herself, or her preferences. In the plainest sense, that was me.

Somewhere along the way, I had decided that instead of revealing my honest thoughts and feelings, I'd stuff them further down, hoping beyond hope they'd find a back door and disappear altogether. To make things easier on everyone, I decided to live behind a mask. That way, I figured, the people around me could see only what they wanted to see—a good daughter, a devoted friend, a loyal coworker, a faithful Christ-follower. And all I would see would be their sheer delight reflected back. It was all so easy and satisfying. The mask covered the pain of my past relationships, my dashed dreams, my unlovable self. The only real challenge was staying creative from behind it. But somehow, I got by.

The mask I wore had its limitations, admittedly. Really sad movies, tender conversations, the probing questions of a gentle friend—these things all created Grand Canyon–sized cracks that I couldn't do anything about. One day, my beloved mask finally gave way and burst into a thousand pieces. But rather than panic, I just produced another one. It was as if I toted them around in my handbag, always at the ready in case the situation necessitated a quick change.

The danger in all of this, as everyone knows,
is that intense serial masking always leads to intense identity crisis.
From age twelve to thirty-three, I lived
with a perpetual false sense of reality.

So, there I sat in the studio that afternoon, exposed and vulnerable, eyeing for the first time the me-behind-the-mask I hadn't seen for decades. Pieces of crumbled jar represented the dreadful debris waiting for me at the bottom of those scary spiral stairs.

MOTION: FREEDOM'S FAULT LINES
21 August 1998

I feel heaviness in my heart. I just keep replaying it like a slow-motion scene from a horror movie, the jar falling apart, shattering to smithereens, right in front of me. As I sat there, watery eyes staring at the scores of jagged pieces, I realized for the first time this so-called jar project was really a Me Project. The piece of artwork most desperately in need of restoration, reformation, was me.

It was a huge moment of impact. Even when I had been trying to chisel the jar, all but insisting the cracks follow the lines I'd drawn, the stubbornness that welled up in my spirit ... when had I become this way? Those hardened places on the jar's belly I kept cursing—Why won't this thickness give way?—those hard places requiring more pressure before they'd surrender, those places were in me. I felt indicted and exposed. And strangely devoid of trust.

Hiding? It was no longer an option. I peered at my artistic rubble-pile, the tiny shards of pottery mocking me in the way they stood for yet another aspect of my sordid past and painful present I couldn't unearth or admit to any human being. I named them as I fingered them, calling them things like, Fear of Rejection, Damaged Goods, Pride, Never to Find True Love, Extreme Hurt, Stubbornness, Fear of Abandonment, Insecurity. It's everything my masks have been hiding, I realized. Before God, before myself, and before others.

Utter disgust over what was true of my life, my identity, washed over me, and I had no clue what to do next. I don't like pain and will do almost anything to avoid it. But now, now I wasn't sure I would even be capable of feeling pain. Could I feel anything? I sat in perfect silence for a long, long time. Seventy-five minutes, at least?

I heard the words—viscerally, almost audibly—"Do you trust Me?"

I said nothing in reply. I wasn't at all sure how to answer.

Over the next two days, I began to ponder that question like never before. Did I *really* trust Him? While I found great comfort behind my mask, I knew that, try though I may, *nothing* was being hidden from God. All those years, He had watched me trudge along the path I had chosen and had been waiting for just the right moment to send this invitation for me finally to face who I am.

He just wasn't going to let me off the hook: He knew that if I wanted to continue collaborating with Him, I simply had to live free. I had to embrace my identity as one created in His image and trust that He would use me for good, despite a boatload of evidence to the contrary.

I needed to be able to create from what was truest of me,
to create from my soul.

Could I trust God to walk me through a process that would throw aside every mask, beat down every wall, and allow me to live life the way He fully intended for me to live? Could I really rely on Him for all the things I considered pipe dreams—contentment and wholeness and acceptance? Really, now, could I?

22 August 1998

This is not easy. In fact, today I'm angry that I ever started this stupid thing. Maybe I won't finish it. It's just too hard. I feel like there are areas that God is asking me to hand over—like being single and being alone and being in need of healing from the wrenching relationships I've been in—but I'm so afraid. Some of the pieces I think He's asking me to hand over, I can't even lift. They're too big. Too awkward. Too heavy. I don't think I can do this. It would be easier to run from it.

I'm not going to the studio today. I'm staying home.

It's just too hard—words I've often said. Backed up by feelings I've often felt. I study my journal entries now and see how absolutely terrified I was to create art not from my surface, but from my soul. It required too great a risk: What if people ridiculed my work—this project that reflected what was truest in me? What if it didn't live up to my friends' expectations? What if I *lost* my friends?

Oswald Chambers says, "When God sends his inspiration, it comes to us with such miraculous power that we are able to arise from the dead and do the impossible. The remarkable thing about spiritual initiative is that the life and power come after we get up and get going. God does not give us overcoming life—He gives us life as we overcome."[1]

Get up and get going. I knew I had to take the first step, risk something, in order to see what God had in store on the other side. I did not want to revisit the past and relive my pain. But that is precisely what God was asking me to do.

COMPLETION: PURSUING THE GOOD "THINGS"
23 August 1998

Something was different this morning. There was a feeling of anticipation. A desire building deep from within. Maybe it's time to stop running. God has continually shown me how faithful He's been at every twist and at every turn. How I wish the same could be said of me.

I drove the five miles to my temporary studio, walked down fifteen stairs, took another look at the pieces still laying lifeless, right where they had fallen four days ago. It was like everything was waiting on me—God, the jar, the air in the room, even. Would I keep going, or would I bail?

I felt calm as I plugged in the glue gun. I took a seat and reached for the first piece. "Fear of Being Alone," I said to it—"that's what we decided to call you the other day, isn't it? Listen, I have a few words for you. My God has said He'll always be with me. You and I … we are going to have to part ways."

It was bolstering to envision myself placing Fear of Being Alone in God's hands and then imagine Him securing the redeemed shard in place. This project— this Me Project—surely will take more than a day to complete. Will I spend a lifetime working through these things, God? I asked silently.

I moved on to the next piece.

My heart raised up, a little lighter, a bit more buoyant than before. Freedom was invading my masked captivity. The jar was taking shape as restoration worked its magic.

I handed over piece after piece, marveling at how God rebuilt the pottery—both the one on the table and the one working on it. "God, I choose to trust You with Pride and Insecurity and Fear of Rejection," I said. "I choose to trust You even with the bane of my existence, Never to Find True Love. I trust You. I really do. Have Your way with all these pieces. I don't want to hold them anymore."

He was patient as I completed my work, never grabbing pieces from me but faithfully receiving them as I lay them in His palm. He didn't ask for me to work a piece in any particular order but seemed to delight in seeing how I would cause things to unfold. This is how trust feels, I thought, feeling God's fingers brush against mine as I handed over what was not mine to hold. Minutes eased into hours. The jar stood, one final shard resting beside its base.

Go ahead, Cindy. It's time we finish this work.

The lights were off, and the shutter whooshed shut-then-open exactly five times as it captured one frame then another—photographs that till now had only had life in my mind.

Two days later, I cradled the black-and-white images of the simple jar that had been smashed to pieces and then magnificently restored. It was complete, for me a tangible manifestation of trust-in-God. That jar had weathered rainstorms, harsh sun rays, and days-on-end of heavy, wet snow, only to find its way into my hands where it then endured two long bouts of cruel and unusual punishment. But today, it sits on my shelf—faint pencil marks as scars—and it is stunning.

And perhaps as far as God is concerned, at least, I am too.

In his book *Orbiting the Giant Hairball*, Gordon MacKenzie says, "You have a masterpiece inside you, too, you know. One unlike any that has ever been created, or ever will be. And remember: If you go to your grave without painting your masterpiece, it will not get painted. No one else can paint it. *Only you.*"[2]

Today, my "masterpiece"—one of the very "good things" God has created for me to do, as Ephesians 2:10 (NLT) talks about—hangs in my office, and whenever I catch sight of it, I am reminded of the one thing God asks of every artist:

Create from what's truest of you, artist.
Create from what's truest of you.

Reflect on your life. What wonderful moments has God
allowed to transpire?
What painful ones?

Have you yet created from the power and emotion and
energy of those moments—all of them?
Is there an emotion or an event that God
is asking you to create from now?

THE CHOOSING-SOUL CRUSADE

Since those jar-project days, I have been on somewhat of a crusade.
A choosing-soul crusade. Admittedly, I continue to struggle with
certain "pieces" that I have to continually hand back over to God—
fears and insecurities and general pillars of stalwarts don't go down
without a fight. But I did experience a freedom during that creative
process like none I had known before. And I crave that freedom for
every artist I meet.

Painters ask me if their paintings are any good, and I say, "Tell
me the story behind it." Writers want an honest assessment, but I
just want one answer: "What compelled you to write about this in
the first place?" Actors' interpretations, musicians' performances,
photographers' compositions—the gauge for how real or effective
or heartfelt or magnificent any of these things are is determined by
the answer to one question only: *Was it created from your soul?*

Like many believer-artists, Carmen was raised in a "Christian
home," the youngest of six children, all who loved to perform. Her
dad, a pastor and also a performer, wrapped spiritual stability and

confidence around the entire family, and as a result, Carmen grew up for the most part happy and well adjusted.

She surrendered her life to Christ at a young age, but it was more of a cultural decision than one born of conviction. "I didn't really feel a tug on my heart," she would later admit, "but it was the right thing to do."

Carmen's passion for dance began around the age of ten. "I don't remember exactly what spurred on my interest," she says. "All I know is that the world of dance seemed to be the most beautiful escape from the painful life-bruises I was racking up."

As she dove deeper into the art form of dance, she required its escape more and more. While she enjoyed the freedom and exhilaration of physical expression, the demands on her body formed bars of a cage that held her relentlessly captive.

"Shortly after my first ballet class—I think I was eleven at the time—I realized I didn't have a 'typical ballerina's body.' Brutally aware of my differences from other, thinner dancers, I did the only thing I could think to do: I began abusing food."

A year into Carmen's battle with a dual-fisted disease—bulimia and depression—the family moved from Chicago to a small town in New Mexico. She entered junior high after that cross-country relocation—"the darkest years of my life," she calls them—and she continued to dance. She also continued to binge and purge.

"Seven months into my time in New Mexico, I started seeing demons everywhere I went," she explains. "By the age of thirteen, I was more afraid than ever. But how was I supposed to tell anyone about the spiritual battle I was in? They'd think I was insane or delusional … or simply a liar."

Carmen kept her private hell to herself, but she began to notice a trend. "The 'demons' that whispered and screamed at me about how horrible a person I was were strangely silent whenever I danced," she said.

After a year in New Mexico, Carmen's family moved once more, this time to Colorado Springs. She struggled to adjust to new surroundings and before long, her bulimia and depression had overtaken her entire life. The whole ugly cycle led her straight into the arms of yet another addiction: cutting. "I was training at a professional ballet school with dozens of beautiful, pencil-thin dancers who were all destined to become prima ballerinas. At the rate I was going," she said, "all I was destined for was suicide."

She took a two-year break from dancing and within a few months of not being in studio was almost fully recovered from bulimia. "I began recovering from my cutting addiction about a year later, when God showed up in new and amazing ways," she said. "He introduced me to several supportive friends, and He gave me a fresh passion for a new artistic avenue, musical theater. I began to settle into myself—my *real* self—trusting Him to guide my steps and heal my wounds."

Carmen's family became involved with our church, and after learning about Carmen's vast creative talent, I invited her to dance on several occasions during worship services and in key roles for special productions. She now says that every rehearsal, every performance, every dance became an opportunity for her to give God glory for everything she had walked through, everything she had survived—the *complete* process. "It took Him bringing me through a dark journey for me to eventually agree to let Him saw through my self-constructed cage," Carmen says. "And while it's the hardest and scariest thing I've ever done,

I've learned that it's only by moving through the struggle
that you find out who you really are."

There's a song by the band Casting Crowns that reminds me of Carmen every time I hear it. One verse begins,

Who am I?
That the eyes that see my sin
Would look on me with love
And watch me rise again

At age sixteen, Carmen values the ability to rise again more than most people I know three times her age. Despite the pockets of pain and areas of struggle she has known, she has been *looked upon with love*, as the song says. And it's from this place that she chooses to create.

I have another friend who has been willing to walk the sometimes-terrifying paces of reflection, motion, completion, in order to create from his soul. He's a singer/songwriter named Jeff, and according to him, the agonizing journey has been worth it, but I'll let you be the judge. Here is his story, in his own words.

Memories are like souvenirs or keepsakes. But more tangible than snow globes or photographs. You don't have to dig through an old box or filing cabinet to find them. In fact, most of the time they dig through you, by way of an autumn breeze, the smell of freshly baked bread, the familiar strains of the radio's song.

So, what would you do if someone came to you today and told you that you are no longer allowed to think about your fondest memories? (As if you could help it, right?) Still worse, what if you were told that whenever you violated the ban—you cheated and snuck in remembrances of a fond memory or two—the thought of them would actually elicit pain and hurt and outright despair instead of the usual elation and joy and spark?

This is what divorce was like for me.

> In the blink of an eye, I had unwittingly joined
> the brotherhood of the broken,
> whose membership requires a ripped-apart heart.

I remember waking up on several occasions in those early months with such an unbearable amount of grief that I would, literally, sit on my floor and think about nothing. Other days, something would trigger a more spiritual response, and I would find all my energies pointed toward God, surprised each time by how very close He seemed. But on an especially dark day, I all but denied my faith. I was swearing and praying and crying and making my bed. Simultaneously. And then a thought entered my mind.

Actually, it was a quote: "Have you considered my servant Job?" (Job 1:8). Initially, I thought, *How cruel of God to do that to Job—to intentionally subject the guy to such unbearable pain!*

According to the story, God tells Satan that he can do whatever he wants to Job and Job will remain steadfast in his faith. And he does. Job asks God a million questions, but you know what God's answer is? Nothing. Actually, God responds, but He basically tells Job that He's God, Job is not, and that's the end of that. Cruel.

As I tossed the pillows back onto my bed that morning, I felt strangely akin to Job: *What if all of this is a test? What if this is more spiritual than I realize?*

In his book *The Problem of Pain*, C. S. Lewis says, "God whispers to us in our pleasures, speaks in our conscience, but shouts in our pain: it is His megaphone to rouse a deaf world."[3] I wrote a song shortly after that bed-making experience called *Pain is a Megaphone.*

> *I'm not saying that there's always something there*
> *I don't claim to know his plans*
> *So when the fiery trials singe your hair*
> *You don't need to understand*
> *But if you're ever slow to hear*
> *You may want to plug your ears*
> *'Cause pain is a megaphone ...*

The song was recorded in my closet, where my clothes served as soundproofing, and is but one track on a sort of Ebenezer-album I just wrapped up called *Okay*. In my life, at least, God indeed has been faithful thus far. In my life, at least, God is the reason I'm doing okay.

Before all this happened—this strange and devastating and spiritual and ugly thing called divorce—I wrote a song for a friend, based on some things he was going through. Partway through that process, I realized that it's really difficult to put myself in someone else's shoes and write what they "must be thinking." Truth be told, at the time, my friend's life seemed more fascinating than the one I was living firsthand, so I decided to tell his tale instead.

> I think a lot of artists struggle with that.
> They want to tell a great story,
> but they are ignorant of their own.

These days, when I find myself pouring out my life over my guitar, tears streaming down my face, wondering where all this emotion is coming from, hoping that this lyric will bring a little more healing to my heart, I feel like I understand the process a little more. Because when the song is finished and playing in someone else's iPod, it somehow winds up healing them. To me, that is art with a capital A.

God has placed everything within us that we'll ever need as artists to create our masterpieces. We can paint the flower on the mountainside and, of course, it will reveal the beauty and majesty of the Designer we know Him to be. But unless *that* flower on *that* mountainside somehow reflects what's truest of *you*—of your journey and your experience and your heartbreaks and your highest highs—can you really call that sort of act *obedience*?

What types of "soul" art have you appreciated from
others? Why was it meaningful to you?
What fears or insecurities sometimes keep you
from creating "soul" art of your own?

-5-

REFLECTIONS IN
THE MIRROR

When Artists Tell Themselves the Truth

"Mirror, mirror on the wall, who's the best artist of us all?"

GROWING UP, I always wanted a talking mirror. You know, like the one the queen had in *Snow White*. How cool I thought it would be to get up in the morning and hear in a thick British accent, "Good morning, Princess Cynthia! My, how lovely you look today!"

Standing there with sleepy eyes, wild bed-head, and wrinkled pajamas, I'm sure I'd smile and say, "Why, thank you! Yes, I *am* lovely, aren't I!"

In reality, my mirror didn't greet me that way at all. Still doesn't. But it does, in fact, talk. Speaking with nonverbals, it reveals wrinkles, it exposes flaws, and it discloses truths too numerous to count. (Perish the thought of someone giving me one that magnifies!)

I despise looking into my mirror as much as the next image-conscious woman, but I also know that avoiding it altogether is not the answer.

> Just because I don't want to see the truth
> about myself at times—
> physically or otherwise—the truth remains the truth.

When it comes to my spiritual development—both as leader and as artist—I owe it to myself, my God, and those whom I lead to stay in touch with the truth. Truly, if I refuse to take a good, hard look into my spiritual mirror every now and again, I'll drift further and further into identity crisis.

Sure, it would be easy to accept affirmation but turn away from anything that's hard to admit about myself, but that approach is hardly effective if I really do want to reflect Christ by manifesting things like humility and obedience and an ever-increasing desire to serve. Which I do.

Francis Schaeffer once said that for all Christians, believer-artists included, "the Christian life itself should be our greatest work of art."[1] It's not that our creative handiwork is unimportant; it's just that our diligent self-work is more important still. Paul defined the by-product of all this "self-work" as lives lived "worthy of the calling we have received," (you do remember my whole invitation spiel, I presume), and defined a person who did so as being "completely humble and gentle … patient, bearing with one another in love" (Eph. 4:1–2).

In the paragraphs that follow, I describe three not-so-nice

reflections I see in my spiritual mirror more frequently than any others, reflections that make me equally crazy with each appearance. They are the bane of the artist's existence, as far as I'm concerned, because their presence kicks the life of "complete humility" and gentle patience to the ground every time. But still, they reflect the truth about who I am on many occasions.

The first of the three reflections deals with an internal struggle, the struggle of ego. The other two deal with how I as an artist relate with people who surround me on the creative journey; namely, criticism and rejection. If you've never seen reflections like these in your mirror, then rest easy in your denial as you flip to chapter 6. But if you have, then read on. And take heart! Christ is committed to transforming the image we *all* see staring back into something a little easier to take.

WHEN THE MIRROR REFLECTS EGO

Toby Keith came out with a song a few years ago that pokes a little fun at self-interest. "I wanna talk about me, wanna talk about I, wanna talk about number one, oh my, me, my …"—I love singing this catchy chorus, but what I don't love is admitting how closely it reflects my heart at times. It's so frustrating to realize how much I *do* want it to be all about me. I want to be right. I want to be in the know. I want to be first. I want to be the best. I want things to go my way.

On those days, all it takes is a passing glance in the spiritual mirror for me to see the rotten fruit of my ego's labor. And based on my experience, I'm not the only artist who struggles with this difficult dynamic.

Validate Me, Please!

Over the years, I've heard the most amazing words fall out of artists' mouths: "I'm not getting enough stage time at this church, so I'm leaving." Or, "I don't understand why I can't sing the lead. I *always* sing lead!" Or, "Please hang my painting by the entrance, okay?" Or, from a guy I'd never even met before, "I just graduated from audio school. Let me tell you how you should mix the sound for this room." At times, I wonder how some of us fit our egos through the door!

There exists a deep longing within every artist to be validated, appreciated, and applauded.

But when artists start to thrive on the next acknowledgment or
accolade,
the next Best in Show,
the next standing ovation,
validation becomes an intoxicating drug that propels them
to crave more
and do more
and say more,
just to feel the next hit.

The only way to keep an ego in check is to follow hard after Jesus Christ, plain and simple. Rather than seeking validation by *being served*—by people's approval, people's praise, people's commendation—He found validation by *serving others*. "For even the Son of Man came not to be served," says Mark 10:45 (NLT), "but to serve others, and to give his life as a ransom for many."

In order to stay grounded and not let our heads become

inflated with "all things us," it is vital that we practice what Christ modeled while He was on this earth. Picking up a towel and filling a basin, God Almighty, the Holy of Holies, stooped to wash the filthy feet of sinners.

King became servant. What a beautiful picture! And as His followers, we are urged to do the same. *This* is the foundation of our calling, to serve instead of seeking to be served—for artists, a Herculean task. To accomplish it,

> We've got to untangle our sense of identity
> from the microphone,
> the paintbrush, the next Top Ten worship song
> and get back in touch with why we do what we do in the first place.

A well-known worship leader once guest-led for our church and carved out time between services on a Sunday morning to meet with our band and vocalists. His first question to everyone was, "Do you know what your spiritual gifts are?"

Yeah, yeah, yeah, I thought. *Encouragement, teaching, leadership … come on, when do we get to talk about worship?*

It seemed a strange question to begin with, but hey, it was his meeting. As some of our team members' heads bobbed up and down, I noticed others sitting silently as if deep in thought.

He went on to share how important it was for artists to know their spiritual gifts, not just their *creative* gifts. For instance, what if you were a singer, and something happened tomorrow to cause you to lose your voice? There would be no more song … so, then what?

What if you were a sound tech and lost your hearing? You could no longer mix sound.

Or, what if you were a guitar hero and suddenly found your hands paralyzed?

What if what made you "you" as an artist was abruptly taken away? Would you still find a way to serve?

Think about your particular art medium,
such as songwriting, photography, dancing,
or painting. If you were told today that you
could no longer pursue it, how would you
respond? How would you continue to serve?

A heavy silence filled the room as one by one, we got real with ourselves about how we'd answer his question if we were forced to be really, really honest.

Above All, Serve

This worship leader explained that artists so often get wrapped up in their creative gifts that they mistake them for spiritual gifts. But nowhere does the Bible list singing, songwriting, painting, dancing, or any of the technical arts when defining the spiritual gifts.[2]

Our team was moved and challenged when we learned that our guest's wife, who has an incredible singing voice, splits her serving time at their church each month by working one weekend onstage behind the microphone, leading people in worship, and the other weekend doing diaper duty in the nursery.

It made me think about what our churches would look like if artists started serving the body from outside the booth, off the stage, and away from the producer's chair. Maybe then, we would have enough children's workers so rooms would not have to be closed down on any given Sunday. Maybe then, the grounds around every church campus would boast colorful flowers instead of pop cans and candy wrappers. Maybe then, guests would always be welcomed, the lonely would always be embraced, and the hurting would always receive prayer. What a place that would be!

If you currently serve one weekend
a month, whether onstage, behind a camera, or in
the sound booth, consider looking for other ways

to serve your church during "off weeks" using your
spiritual gifts, rather than merely your creative gifts.

I sat there that Sunday morning and just wondered what
would transpire if we all picked up towels and started to wash
the feet of those around us in our daily lives, even in the smallest
of ways. It was easy to stand in judgment of everyone else on the
team—like, *Hey, yeah! Why don't they do more to help out around
here!*—but then my finger pointed toward me.

It occurred to me that while I was more than willing to serve
in ways large and small, I was still pretty attached to my artistic
contributions. I couldn't imagine not having my eyes to create
colorful stage designs or capture special moments with my camera,
my ears to assess songs, my hands to manipulate video editing
equipment. I *was* struggling with his question. My mind was saying, *Sure, I'd keep serving*, but my heart was doing a double take.
Would I? Would I *really* continue to serve?

Of course, I long to play a part in building God's kingdom
and have no intention of sitting on the sidelines, but the question
prompted an interesting round of introspection.

Two days after that morning meeting, I realized I needed a few
things from the grocery store. I pulled into a parking spot just
as a thunderstorm erupted overhead, and as I raced toward the
entrance, I noticed a young mom putting the last bag of groceries

in the back of her SUV. A toddler stood beside her with his little hands over his head as he tried to shield himself from the rain. About that time, I caught sight of a big, heavy cast on the woman's right foot.

She shut the trunk door, looked down at her son, and then looked toward the front of the store, as if wondering how she could return the cart without leaving her son stranded in the rain. I rushed over and said I'd be happy to take the cart inside for her, an offer that was met with a relieved smile.

Sure, it wasn't diaper duty, but the small gesture brought back the reminder to serve in the little things. *Above all, serve.* It's what came to my mind that day in the pouring rain, and it's what gets rebranded on my heart each time I consider Christ's selfless, egoless example.

These days, when I hear someone ranting about not getting enough "stage time," I kick them in the shin. Okay, not really. But I do recommend three or four other serving opportunities that exist right then, right there, within our church body. If they're not interested, then I know it's time to sit down and ask them why they're here to begin with. Being an artist is not about demanding diva status. It's about serving. Period.

WHEN THE MIRROR REFLECTS CRITICISM

There are days when all I can see staring back at me in my mirror is criticism. Which would be fine, except that to an artist, criticism is not only an attack on her art; it's also an attack on her person. If we're not careful, artists walk around, thin-skinned and paranoid, believing there's a caustic critic around every corner. Call me crazy, but I think God has something altogether different in mind when He invites us to collaborate with Him.

I came across a book one time titled *Creative Sparks*,[3] which contains a hundred and fifty artist-oriented vignettes and claims to ignite your design ingenuity. One of my favorites is called "Heat," and says this: "The ability to gracefully withstand the heat of criticism is no less important than the artistic skill [artists] bring to a project. When an artist appears unwilling to consider suggestions from clients and peers, they run the risk of being perceived as defiant, lofty."

Author Jim Krause then challenges the artist to "learn to hold the ego in a state of suspension when your work is being reviewed. Remember, a critic doesn't need to know as much as you do about design in order to spot a weakness or mistake."[4]

Learn to hold the ego in a state of suspension—if only it were always that easy! I believe the reason artists have such a tough time accepting and assimilating criticism is that they become so closely connected to their art that to hear a comment that is anything but glowing and loving enters their universe as a creativity-crasher.

On more than a few occasions, I've been hip deep in design-mode, working feverishly to complete a graphic. Just when I catch a glimpse in my mind's eye of what the final piece will look like and charge off in that direction to bring it to completion, someone inevitably walks by my office, spots what's on my computer screen, and says, with incredible helpfulness in their voice, "That's not *done* yet, is it?"

The tiny hairs on the back of my neck rise to attention every time. Pasting a smile on my face, I spin around in my chair and reply through gritted teeth, "No, I'm still working on it. But thank ... you ... for ... your ... interest." (*Now, beat it!*)

No Shortage of Opinions

Early on, handling criticism was an impossible task for me. As I've confessed, I'm a people-pleaser at heart, and I was simply unwilling to accept the fact that I really couldn't please all three thousand worship-service attendees at our church. Instead of learning how to filter the comments that came in following each weekend, I wore them on my person as layer upon layer of discouragement.

"Why can't we sing more hymns?"

"The music is too loud."

"The music is too soft."

"Why can't we hear the vocals? Turn down the band."

"The worship leader's shirt needed to be ironed. And could he please tuck it in next week?"

"Drums, drums, drums ... are the natives getting restless or something?!"

"The pastor sounds tinny. And when he gets reflective, he whispers. I can barely hear a word he says."

"The outfit on the singer was too tight. This isn't a bar, you know."

And on and on it goes. I have come to the conclusion after a decade in full-time ministry that as long as church work involves people, there will be no shortage of opinions.

I recently asked a close friend and our church's technical director (the "sound guy") how he handles criticism so well. He admitted that, on most days, he's able to hear what the individual is saying with a clear mind and a clean heart. He checks for the kernel of truth in their input, and if they're correct in their assessment, he makes the necessary adjustments and moves on. If they're wrong, he dismisses the critique without taking it personally and goes about his business as usual. I sit two feet from him in the sound booth each weekend, and still this noble spirit hasn't rubbed off on me!

Well, *mostly* noble. The filter he uses is indeed helping him get better at handling opinions and objections, but he openly admits that at times he tosses it out the window in favor of adopting a posture of sheer disillusionment and despondency. I kind of grin every time I see it happen: He isn't always perfect, which gives the rest of us hope to walk on.

Criticism's Upside

While I'm still working on the holding-the-ego-in-suspension thing when negative comments come my way, I have at least matured enough in my development as an artist and a leader to recognize criticism's undeniable upside. One day—an especially miserable day when it seemed everyone was engaged in target practice and I had the bulls-eye painted on my forehead—I looked up the word *critic*. Webster told me that it was a noun that meant, "one who appraises the merit of other's works, especially artistic or literary."[5]

Somehow, it comforted me to think of the marksmen around me as "artistic appraisers," all who seek excellence as much as I do. All who desire the church's relevance as much as I do. All, I choose to believe, who want God to get glory as much as I do. When I allow myself to receive criticism in this spirit, I am beautifully stretched inside. My heart gets expanded. My pride gets tempered. And my focus gets recast to where it should have been all along: on the one Artist who needs no critique, Jesus Christ.

WHEN THE MIRROR REFLECTS REJECTION

My friend's little boy, Luke, has an interesting response to being told no. He growls. But it's not just any growl. It's the ugliest, most awful, snarling sound you've ever heard. It starts at his toes, courses through his veins, and winds up in the back of his throat. The sheer force of it causes his nose to flip skyward and his arms to flail. I'm never exactly sure what he's thinking about in the thick of those moments, but all indications are that he could eat his mother.

It's all well and good and adorable in a little five-year-old body. It's *not* so cute when you're supposed to be a sophisticated, Spirit-filled adult.

Recently, I had the experience of watching a similar (albeit a *tad* more civilized) growl-fest unfold over the course of an entire year in the life of an artist whom I dearly love.

My friend had auditioned for a role in an upcoming production

at our church, a role she'd played on several occasions in years
past. When she found out that someone else got the part this time
around, she was shocked and hurt. So, to deal with her disap-
pointment and pain, she decided to just "be done." (Growl.) There
would be no more acting. (Growl.) She said there would be no
more auditions. (Growl.) There would be no more *artist*. (Growl.)
In fact, while she was at it, she decided she might as well leave the
ministry altogether. So, no more church, too. (*Big* growl.)

Feeling completely justified in this string of actions, she proceeded to pull herself out of all things pertaining to the arts and told
me by phone that she would be "moving on to something else."

A few days passed, and I guess the initial sting of rejection began
to wear off a little. My friend started thinking about how her behav-
ior would look to the rest of the cast, the director, the ministry team,
and, most importantly, to Christ. She finally surrendered herself to
God's healing ways and allowed Him to soothe the places that hurt
with His supernatural balm. In the end, rather than ditching her role
as an artist, she chose to take the high road instead.

Opening night of the production came, and as the house lights
dimmed in our church's auditorium, she and her husband took
their seats—on the front row, even—and supported the cast with
rapt attention. When the final scene was over, they wore genuine
smiles and gave the actors a round of heartfelt applause.

A Better Role to Play

My friend who had been rejected for the part in the play told
me recently that those were some of the most difficult days she'd ever
walked through as an artist, those ambiguous days of questioning

God, questioning the people who had seemingly rejected her, questioning her capabilities as an actor. She now sees that God was working even in the midst of the ambiguity, though. She didn't get the part she auditioned for, but she did get the role that God had written just for her. The role was called Mom.

The hours she would have spent memorizing lines or participating in rehearsals she redirected toward her son, who happened to be walking through a really difficult situation several hundred miles away. In the end, they logged hours on the phone that she never would have had time or energy for had she landed the role she thought she wanted. The invitation to more present parenting was a different invitation than the one she thought she deserved, but the key was that she willingly said yes to the one that *did* come her way.

Sometimes, God answers our prayers with a clear yes or no. But sometimes, it's a little fuzzier than that. I've learned that sometimes His "no" simply means "wait." Perhaps it's not the right season for something we think we want. Or maybe we're not quite prepared for whatever God has in store for us. He needs to refine us a little more before we jump into a particular blessing. In my artist-friend's case, God obviously knew she needed some extra margin in order to be there for her son. He knew *that* was the role she needed to play.

I've had my fair share of nos through the years, and, like every other artist, I've wrestled through a few defining moments regarding how I would handle them. Most recently, I was told no after I worked to get a few of my photographs published in an artist directory. I knew it was a long shot, but still, I felt compelled to complete the application form and mail in the entry fee.

Ninety days passed before a letter arrived in the mail. "Thank you for your recent submissions for our call to entry," it began. "There were over 1,800 entries submitted, and we could only choose 300. While we loved your work, and the decision was extremely difficult, your artwork has not been chosen...."

Growl.

I sat on the couch reading and rereading the letter, telling myself that everything was going to be okay. But inside, the pricks of pain were striking deep. I thought about the hundreds of times I'd tried to encourage artists when they found out they'd been rejected from this art show or that audition. Oh, how my inspiring words were coming back to haunt me now!

The next day, I told my friend Betsy about the letter and how I had been denied for the directory. She lovingly said, "Hey, you don't know the whole story. Maybe your piece was number 301, and you were only one image away from being chosen!"

Her words didn't help, but had I been in her shoes, I likely would have said the same thing.

Supplying Your Best

When artists get rejected, the tendency is to behave like "little Lukes," growling, snarling, arms flailing, the whole bit. *Can you believe it?* we think. *The nerve of them, saying I'm not good enough! How dare they! What gives them the right to decide whether or not my art is praiseworthy?* Or, *What was the director thinking? Didn't he see how awful those other auditions were?*

We spend every last ounce of energy finger-pointing and blame-casting and resolve in our minds and hearts that we're never going to create again. *I'll show them!* (Whoever "they" are.) *I'll stop painting! Stop auditioning! Stop singing! Stop creating altogether!* If the downward spiral isn't arrested, it can lead us to ever-worsening levels of bleakness and despair. Frustration turns to anger, anger turns to bitterness, and bitterness hardens a heart. And *you* try creating something God-honoring with a hardened heart! It's just not possible.

There are two questions I'm learning to ask when I find myself stung by rejection. The first is, *Did I supply my very best?* Was it the best painting I could have painted? The best song I could have sung? The best performance I could have given? The best arrangement I could have played? If so, then I rest in the fact that, while people's opinions of my work may have been unenthusiastic, I honored God by being obedient to creating my very best creation. And that, for me, was enough.

When was the last time you received a
"no" regarding your art?

Had you prepared adequately?
Was it your "best" work at that time?
How did you respond upon being told no?
What lessons did you learn as a result?

The second question is, *Will God supply His very best?* Either God is faithful to keep His promises, or He is not. Believing He is faithful means I can cling to His commitment to prosper me, provide for me, make a way for me, and lift me up. Regardless if my art is rejected or not.

Ephesians 4:30–31 says, "Do not grieve
the Holy Spirit of God....Get rid of all bitterness,
rage and anger, brawling and slander, along
with every form of malice." Where are your
opportunities for growth in this regard?

WHEN THE MIRROR REFLECTS CHRIST

A friend of mine who is a worship leader recently handed me the lyrics to a new song he'd written called "More of You." My heart was more steadied with each line read. "When I'm lost in need of mercy," the song began, "more of you, more of you. When I've wasted time you've given, more of you, more of you. When I've taken more than giving, more of you, more of you. And when I leave before you've spoken, more of you, more of you."

It went on this way, declaring with each phrase that, no matter how I have messed up, the one and only thing that will set it all right again is more of Jesus, more of Jesus. "When I've wandered from your presence ... as I find my way to mercy ... when I'm scared in need of clinging ... when I'm cold in need of holding ... as I bring this life that's broken ... when I leave before you've spoken, more of you, more of you."[6]

Truly, neither you nor I can muster the strength to serve others instead of serving our own egos, the willingness to submit to input when all we see is *criticism* with a capital C, or the security of knowing that rejection must flee when we've supplied our best, unless we put off self and put on *more of God*. It's the only way to get the mirror's reflection to showcase not us, but Christ.

In my day-to-day life, I possess such a deep desire to get things right. (I've mentioned this to you, yes?) I want to be perfect, to create perfect art that God can use to change lives, to walk in perfect humility, to serve with a perfect spirit, to be perfectly obedient, and yet I rarely make it to noon without screwing up in a half dozen different ways. I get defensive. I brush off colleagues' needs. I run too far ahead on a project without asking for directions.

I. I. I. When all the time, what I really need is more of *God*.

Clare of Assisi, one of the first followers of Francis of Assisi, once said to the artist: "Place your mind before the mirror of eternity! Place your soul in the brilliance of glory! Place your heart in the figure of divine substance! And transform your whole being in to the image of the Godhead itself through contemplation."[7] But how do I get there? How do *you* get there? How do we look in the mirror and see more of him and less of us? How do we help usher in that day when ego and insecurity (not to mention, bed-head) will be no more? How do we prove out Paul's promise in 2 Corinthians 3:18, that we, "who with unveiled faces all reflect the Lord's glory, are being transformed into his likeness with ever-increasing glory, which comes from the Lord, who is the Spirit"?[8]

Let me give you three ideas. As you read them, ask God to show you where to begin in your own practice of spiritual discipline.

Be Still

Sometimes, I enjoy sitting in my favorite chair, leaning my head back, and taking in deep breath after deep breath. In and out, in and out—I'm aware of my breathing and aware of my *being*. Stop your *doing* momentarily, friend, and just be. Wait for your blood pressure to drop a little, and then quietly—silently, even—ask God if He's okay with who you are. With your *being*. What would He tweak if you gave Him free reign? Sit a spell in His presence and listen for His still, small voice. All your "doing" later on will thank you for it.

Saturate Your Mind

There is no better book on the face of planet Earth than God's holy Word. You can trust it, you can learn from it, and you can live it out. Perfectly inerrant, supernaturally informative, endlessly and timelessly able to be implemented—is there any other resource that can make these claims? When I open the Scriptures and consider the amazing chase God has been on since before the start of time to reclaim us as His own, I am humbled and awed all over again. Read your Bible. There and there alone, you will find comfort, healing, guidance, wisdom, and peace.

Replay the Tapes

After a particularly intense day or week or month or year, one of the most centering tasks I engage in is to replay the tapes of my experience: Who was involved? What happened? How did I feel about it? Are there any loose ends I need to tie up as a result of it?

Every once in a while, take stock. Write it down, speak it out, or simply let it well up inside you. As you seek to make sense of conversations and occasions, challenges and opportunities, be reminded that, as Isaiah 44:24 promises, God is your Lord, who made all things. He alone stretched out the heavens. Nobody was with Him when He made the earth. He is big! He is able! He will celebrate over you when the mountaintop surfaces under your feet, and He will turn ashes to beauty when the bottom falls out.

Thank Him for it all—blue skies that lift your spirit, second chances that renew your hope, cranky clerks who remind you to be the kindness of Christ wherever you go. In no time at all, you'll gaze into that mirror of yours and grin a knowing grin at the sight of the Jesus in you, shining through and through.

More of You, Jesus, more of You.

Using a piece of blank paper or your journal, draw an
image that reflects where you see yourself right now in
terms of your artistic journey (stick figures are allowed).
Consider questions such as,
- Am I carving out time to create art?
- Do I seize training and development opportunities to
keep my skills sharp?
- Am I plugged into community with other artists?
- Is my influence helping other artists
to say "yes" to God too?

On another page, draw where you would like to be
this time next year. Then, every month or two, pull out
that drawing and assess the progress you have made.
Trust God to give you a clear picture of the path He has
you on, as well as the vision for who you will become
as an artist if you remain faithful to saying yes.

~6~
TWO ARE BETTER THAN ONE

Choosing the Course of Collaboration

Two are better than one ...
—ECCLESIASTES 4:9

For my teammates, past and present:
Annie, Brandon, Bridget, Chelsea, Dave, Don,
Elaine, Gary, Geri, Jason,
Jeff, Jim, John, Josh, Kaye, Kevin, Liz, Mark S.,
Mark St., Mark T., Mike, Nate, Neilin,
René, Ron, Rian, Scott, Sheryl, Steve, and
Tammy

THURSDAY, I RECEIVED a job offer. This doesn't happen to me every Thursday, so that day kind of set itself apart from all the other Thursdays I have known.

A pastor from a growing, thriving, wonderful church in Nashville contacted me and shared the church's brief history and explained that they're at a crossroads—do they hire a full-fledged worship pastor, or do they add a creative director instead? He talked about the talented artists in his church and said that, more than a particular title, his folks needed a specific competency. They needed a leader who could unite the team so that they could successfully move their church ahead in the creative vision they believed God had given them.

We talked about my philosophy on the arts and the role I believe artists should play in the local church. We talked about my take on worship and, more the case, on leading people into a posture of worship. And then, we got to my thoughts on the issue of team.

Team. Not "team," as in annoying clichés like "There's no 'I' in 'team'" or "Together Everyone Achieves More," but team, as in spiritual family members banding together to chase a pulse-racing, competency-expanding, God-given goal. Team, as in the Bible's promise that two are always better than one.

I got to the end of my little diatribe, and as I began to exhale, Mr. Growing-Thriving-Wonderful asked if I wanted the job. The Very Large Job. For Very Small Me. Didn't he know I was just a farm girl from Missouri and that it probably wasn't even legal for me to dream dreams this big? Didn't he know that I'd just celebrated ten years of service with my current church and that I couldn't just take the accolades and the cake and run, for crying out loud? Didn't he know that we were mere inches away from hiring a new worship pastor of our own? For me to bail now would surely be considered poor form by everyone I knew and respected.

My mind whirred in erratic patterns, but I pulled myself together long enough to say what all good Christians say in such situations: "I'll pray about it."

"Well, why don't we do that right now?" he asked.

And with that, my bluff had been called.

Don't get me wrong: I really was going to pray about it. Just not right then. With him on the phone. I breathed a sigh of relief when he explained that, most of all, he wanted to pray for me. Which meant I could just sit quietly and show none of my cards.

Over the eight minutes that followed, I listened intently while words of life poured forth from his mouth, as if through a funnel positioned directly over my heart. I pressed my ear tighter and tighter to the phone's handset as he thanked God for my gifts and the way He'd created me. He thanked God for our mutual friend in Tennessee who had crossed our paths. He thanked God for our two churches— separated by two states but uncannily bound by our kindred spirit in Christ. And he thanked God, who had already gone before us in this decision and who was willing to tell us what steps to take, if only we would ask.

We ended the phone call with a promise to talk in two weeks. I leaned back in my office chair, all alone and deeply rattled. I hadn't expected the call to be as meaningful as it had been, and suddenly, the firm ground I'd been standing on seemed altogether wobbly. I let my eyelids fall, bowed my head, and said, "God, I'm overwhelmed. Would You please give me a grateful heart regarding where I am and a wise course of action regarding where to go from here?"

And then I had a sixty-second panic attack, stopped short only because I heard the voices of two of my teammates who were passing by my office in the adjacent hallway. We often joke that if you really want to get something accomplished in our department, just stand in the intersection where all the hallways in our area meet. It's the most profitable seven square feet of the entire facility because as soon as you enter it, you somehow morph into a generous and gregarious traffic cop, happy to point teammates in whatever direction they need to go.

I hurriedly brushed tears from my cheeks in case they were headed my way and, once composed, sat quietly as I listened to their prattle, their laughter, their joy, from my side of the paper-thin wall. Reflexively, I smiled. I thought back on the fond memories we'd shared as a team, and with each recollection, I realized God was already answering the "grateful heart regarding where I am" part of my prayer.

Early on, my teammates summoned my trust enough to help me strip away the many masks I wore. These were the ones who would come to know me better than I knew myself, in many ways. When I'd pushed things too far and neglected self-care, they'd show up in my office, armed with mandates to take time off. When my creative muscles were flabby and tired, they'd cover for me and save the day—regardless which day needed saving. In my bluer moments, when I couldn't take another step, my phone would ring and their encouraging words of truth and life and hope would penetrate my depressed and sad, sad state.

During various ministry seasons, when all
roads seemed to lead to
transition hell and I didn't think I could muster
the courage or conviction
to face one more organizational change,
they rallied around our worship-arts vision
again and again,
declaring one more time that,
even as we found ourselves in shifting sands,
our calling had not shifted, not one iota.

We'd done life together. We'd celebrated birthdays, anniversaries, holidays, and vacation time together. We'd prayed for each others' friends to surrender their lives to God and watched with amazed glee as those lives actually got transformed. We'd met for sunrise service run-throughs at the crack of dawn, sat in Scrooge auditions till midnight, and on various occasions laughed and fought and pouted and cheered nearly every hour in between.

We had done all these things—my team members living proof that two are indeed better than one. We'd operated hand in glove for exactly a decade. And now, I was contemplating walking away.

I had gotten about this far in my reminiscing when one of my team members burst into my office with a fifteen-point list of questions regarding the weekend's stage setup. Life and death stuff, you know.

Still, letting the Nashville call blur out of focus, I felt myself tense up, as if this teammate's concerns were the absolute most important concerns I had ever heard articulated by another human being. I wanted him to have everything he could possibly need in order to do his part of the work effectively, efficiently, and with as little stress as possible. I was his leader, he was part of my team, and the only thing that was going to happen on my watch was excellence.

The phone interview had left me drained and daydreamy, but as I forged ahead through meetings with various team members all afternoon, I noticed the usual conversations now carried with them a special urgency. It was something akin to how I felt during the days after my uncle Kenny had abruptly died. I sat with my family in the stifling Missouri heat, watching snapshots on a DVD fade from one to another of Kenny fishing himself into sunburned oblivion on his beloved boat. With Kenny now gone, my eye picked up details of those old photos I'd never before studied. The faded green shirt he wore whenever he was on the water. The salt-and-pepper shades of gray surrounding the temples of his hairline. The way he squinted every time he smiled. I wished I'd been more present while he was present. With the prospect of saying good-bye to my team now on the table, I resolved to pay more careful attention to them in the here and now.

A meeting with my administrator was next on my agenda for the day. He shared his concerns about how to help our artists understand the importance of serving throughout the next ministry year. He handed me an article he was working on that would deploy in our next online ministry newsletter, and for the umpteenth time, I gave thanks to God for this faithful man's friendship and partnership.

After that, I got word that another team member had received her cancer test result: It was negative. I hugged her a little tighter and told her how thankful I was for her presence and her service to our ministry.

The next day, I went in early to check on one of our video coordinators who had just bought his first house. Earlier that afternoon, his entire family had flown to Colorado. It was their first time to see the state, as well as their new home. He needed to be with them, but the weekend's two video projects still needed his undivided attention. We recapped briefly the creative vision of each project and then, upon discovering he needed a few more stills for one piece, I offered to jump on the Web to do some research for him. It was the least I could do: His eyes betrayed his weariness, and I knew he had but two things on the brain: Get home. See my family! We were in this together, and rather than growing frustrated that his focus was personal instead of professional, I found myself wonderfully humbled that I was able to be part of his team and part of his art. Two are better than one.

I got home that night, doused a salmon filet with olive oil and minced garlic—it's the one thing I actually know how to cook—tossed the pan into a warm oven, headed upstairs to be reunited with my beloved sweatshirt, and tried to shift mental gears to the one thing I needed to accomplish before sunrise the next day: writing this chapter. It was supposed to be on "the power of team," according to my editor, and although the day had organically produced a twelve-point thesis on knowing, serving, loving, and sticking with your team, all I could do when I opened my laptop's lid was sit and stare at the blinking cursor. Fearing being sworn at by that editor-person, I finally corralled my thoughts, the first of which took me to the origin of the team idea.

WHY A TEAM?

Ecclesiastes 4:9 says that the reason two are so much better than one is that two have "a good return for their work."

> Two people can cover each other's weaknesses,
> highlight each other's strengths,
> carry each other's burdens,
> and enable each other to soar.

But one person just has to go it alone, hoping and praying people will love him in spite of himself. Sure, I have a spiritual gift or two on my own, but the purpose of my giftedness is that it may be used in community in order to produce a better return on my work than if I galloped through life as the Lone Ranger. If anyone could have gotten away with a rescue-the-situation-and-then-ride-off-in-the-sunset spirit, it was God. And yet He refused to operate as a renegade isolationist. Father, Son, and Holy Spirit: The Trinity exists together, works together, creates together, communes together always. And we are created to do the same.

When we were kids, my younger brother, Steve, had one of those Mr. Potato Head toys, complete with fifteen thousand tiny body parts and accompanying accessories. I'd watch him sit on our living room floor with potato body in hand and remove its eyes, nose, ears, lips, and arms. He'd then see how many different faces he could make by adding a mustache to its ear, a pipe to its belly, or a new and different hat to the top of its head.

When he would get bored, he'd ditch the potato to move on to other, more exciting toys, and I'd take his spot. (Quietly, of course, since no self-respecting preteen would be caught dead playing with plastic vegetable people. The toy was for *children*, a group to which I did not belong, thank you very much.)

Despite my wacky potato-head concoctions that would have inspired Picasso himself, the thing I think of most when I recall those days is Paul's concept from 1 Corinthians 12. He talks about how ridiculous it would be if our ears said, "Because I am not an eye, I do not belong to the body," (v. 16) or how useless it would be if the entire body were an eye. Who would do our hearing for us? Likewise, if we were one giant ear, how would we smell a rose?

His exact words in that verse read: "The body is a unit, though it is made up of many parts; and though all its parts are many, they form one body" (1 Cor. 12:12). And he's not just referring to a physical body, but also to a spiritual body. So, this is how we're supposed to function as teams, with unity, in formation, as one body.

The idea begs some good questions for the leader of artists: When an outside person looks at my team (myself included), do they see a "well-formed body"? Do they find everything in its place—the eyes resting above the nose, blinking like they were made to blink; the ears perched on the side of the head, open and ready to hear; hands hanging at the end of arms, feet steady under the ends of legs; the spine going up and down instead of side to side?

List the names of your team members, and beside each
name, write down which part of the "unified body"
that person represents. Maybe someone serves as the
eyes for your team, always watching for pitfalls. Or
perhaps they are the ears, always listening for input
that will sharpen the group. Is someone your team's
helpful hands; their strong and steady voice; their
active feet; their caring soul; their thinking mind?
Jot down your perceptions and then share them with
your team members during your next team meeting.
In His deliberate design, God
"arranged the parts in the body,
every one of them,
just as he wanted them to be" (v. 18).

God combined the members of the body so there would be
no division. All are equal and yet need each other to function as
one body.

MY TOP TEN REGARDING TEAM

If David Letterman phoned me and said that his list-writer was
down with a stomach bug and asked if I could please present a Top

Ten on, say, teamwork, I'd nail my television debut, no problem. But on the heels of my acceptance, I'd have to confess that my list didn't come from me. It came, ironically enough, from my team— the same team that teaches me every day how to operate more and more as a unified body. The same team that, understandably, I'm having trouble potentially leaving.

In the past decade, my team members have led me, they have taught me, and they have stretched me. They have loved well, they have served well, and they have, above all, worshipped well through their countless acts of obedience to God, time and again saying yes to the Grand Invitation-Giver. Here is what I have learned as my team's admiring student, in Top Ten fashion:

Number ten: You're not perfect. I know this must be a colossal bubble-burst (it was for me), but it's the truth. We all have weaknesses and days when our "game isn't on," which is a nice way of saying you're unbearable and nobody wants to be around you. This is when DOG days are needed most. Days Of Grace foster the willing spirit that says, "I will step in for you, I will cover for you, I will love you where you are, and I will ask nothing in return."

Nine: Plans must be held loosely. God has a way of changing our minds. And, as a result, our plans. As a leader of artists, you get too emotionally attached to the "But we decided …!" framework, and you're toast.

Eight: Laughter is from God. Any artist team must be able to laugh with each other. And sometimes, *at* each other. (Ours tends to have an overabundance of the latter, truth be told.)

Seven: Admit when you are wrong, even when you are absolutely sure it will kill you. Enough said on that.

Six: Keep short accounts. If something happens between teammates, all parties must be willing to ask forgiveness and start again. (Oh, how my nonconfrontational self has kicked and screamed against this exhortation, but I now acknowledge it as a must for healthy team functionality.)

Five: Authenticity starts with the leader. (Isn't that the worst thing you have ever read? Like, why can't authenticity be a grassroots effort that winds up with me? But alas, it doesn't work that way.) Your team will not operate from a place of authenticity unless you first choose to do so.

Four: We must be willing to speak the truth in love. Then, we must actually do it. Effective leaders insist on doing both.

Three: We must always serve.

Two: We must consistently pray.

And, drum roll, please ... number

One: We must selflessly love.

Most days, my team members reflect two things that were true even for the original artisans, Oholiab and Bezalel. They reflect specific, God-given gifts, and they reflect an insatiable desire to put those gifts to work for God's glory.

But that's only *most* days.

Lest you think I perpetually dance through fields of daisies, hands of teammates held on either side, I should divulge three other things my team has taught me, three that aren't quite as noble or delightful to discuss as the previous ten.

Reality 1: We All Carry Baggage

One morning recently, I was part of a meeting that included teams from three different ministry departments. We were coming together to brainstorm an upcoming sermon series, (on serving, ironically). As each person entered the room, all sorts of luggage entered with them.

The baggage—family history, life experiences, strengths, weaknesses, dreams, disappointments, nuances of complex spiritual journeys—was too heavy, too tightly packed, too tightly held.

Ten minutes in, I doubted we'd accomplish anything worthwhile. But it was crucial that we get on the same page and make some progress, and so we persevered. After a few awkward exchanges, several simple phrases told me the collective unpacking had begun. Phrases like "One time we did …" or "Hey, what about using …" or "You know, we could …" I listened in amazement as those from my team probed the others' thoughts, asking follow-up questions like "Can you tell us more about that?" or "What was the effect of using that approach?"

Great questions, all.

By the time we were done, the white board reflected three dozen colorful ideas and two powerful courses of action we could pursue, proving once more that collaboration works. We had walked in not knowing what we were in for, but had submitted to a creative process—even one that was highly honoring, interpersonally—that allowed us to dream loftier dreams, think deeper thoughts, and eventually get our hearts to sing off the same sheet of music.

With the arrival of every artist—every team member—appears a set of luggage. Sometimes it takes weeks, months, or even years of walking in grace with each other to fully unpack it, but as a leader of artists, part of your role is to help shoulder the baggage until that time. It doesn't mean you claim it as your own. But it does mean you acknowledge it, you help your teammates carry it, and you work like mad to help unpack it so that the group's load gets lightened.

Reality 2: We're Selfish to the Core

When my sister and I were young, our place in the family car was always the backseat. She sat on one side, I'd sit on the other, and in between us sat the thick and impenetrable Line. It may have been invisible, but its presence was crystal clear to us at all times.

The Line meant that she had her space and I had mine. We could look at each other, but heaven forbid if one of our legs crossed the Line because we'd immediately yell, "Maaaah-ahm, she's not staying on her side!" My mom would calmly remind us that she was quite willing to turn the car around, don't think she wouldn't do it.

I loved that Line because it allowed me my own little kingdom, complete with its own little princess—me. But somewhere along the way, the Line lost its luster. No longer did it merely divide pipsqueak sisters who wanted a little uninterrupted time with their Barbies, but entire groups who wanted nothing to do with each other. Left to our own devices, we're selfish to the core, whether that core is Republican or Democrat, union member or staff management, Broncos fan or Chiefs fan, war proponent or pacifist, seeker or believer.

Perceptions become fact, which then becomes truth ... period. We don't work to obtain all the other angles before we make our minds up that our angle is right. Over the years, our worship-arts team has worked hard to break down the silos and erase every invisible Line that exists even between our own teams, but it has been far from easy.

During my early days in ministry, I remember sitting in a Saturday-afternoon rehearsal to try to get my arms around this thing called arts leadership. From my auditorium seat, I could see both the stage and our sound booth. I was observing the team onstage and the team running in and out of the sound booth, when something in my mind prompted me to focus a little more intently on the team members themselves.

That's when I saw it: the good, old invisible Line.

It had been drawn with the fattest of black markers, right between those onstage and those in the booth.

Selfish, snide remarks flew back and forth as band members demanded different monitor mixes and technicians passed knowing glances to each other. Onstage, vocalists worked on their three-part harmony while, at the same time, the bass player practiced his new riff. He was in his own world, oblivious to band requests and worship leader cues alike. Which made it tough for the booth guys to hear what they were being asked to do.

It was sheer chaos that culminated in one of the vocalists stomping off the stage as he mumbled something about going back and adjusting the monitors himself. (*Not exactly* what Paul had in mind with his whole "operate in fluid unity" spiel.)

Sixty minutes later, I saw this same group of people put on happy-masks and walk onstage to lead the congregation in a meaningful time of worship. To an outsider, I'm sure everything looked and felt like a normal worship service, but armed with the knowledge of how the process had unfolded to get them to that point, I decided radical change was in order.

As we work to build God's kingdom, God's artists must find paths to selflessness. It's not easy for any Christ-follower, but for creative types who are quite accustomed to self-sufficiency, the task can be especially arduous. Here's why it matters:

Every weekend, no matter how large or how
small the congregation,
individuals walk through the front doors
seeking one thing: answers.
Answers to deep questions like,

Why did my spouse leave?
Why does my body hurt this way?
Why are my finances such a wreck?
Is peace really something I can find?
Does God know I exist?
Does He care?

We owe them our very best answers, born from our very best efforts to reflect the kindness of Christ in a fractured, fallen world.

When you and your team members fight for fluid unity, God says He'll give you a good return for your work. So, where to begin? I recommend doing what our team did—talk to the One who invented the concept to begin with, God Himself.

A couple of weeks after that, on the heels of a Saturday-afternoon rehearsal, I asked the team to convene near the stage area. And I wanted them all—worship leaders, band members, vocalists, camera operators, lighting and sound techs, video directors, and the producer for that weekend's services (which was me).

I asked them to listen carefully as various team members shared their insights about the service. What did they hope God would do? What lyrics or skit lines were most meaningful to them and why? How did they want attendees to feel after it was all said and done? After several people talked through their impressions, we all grabbed hands and prayed. (Still no dancing through daisies, but it was a start.)

We prayed for clear minds and united hearts. We prayed to exhibit selfless attitudes and servant-minded gestures. We prayed for anointed worship, transformational teaching, and overall, a Spirit-led service.

Over the months, cool things began to happen as a result of our team's faithfulness to prayer. Each person saw how he or she fit into the bigger worship-arts picture. Band members started talking with the sound guys. Vocalists engaged a few band members. The stage artists began relating to the technical artists. Eventually, we arrived at the place where "we" could head into each service with arms—and spirits—linked. It didn't mean we had defeated our selfish tendencies altogether. It just meant we were getting better and better at momentarily trumping them with unity.

Reality 3: Collaborators Are Inherently Annoying

Although I'm a raving advocate of collaboration philosophically, I'm not always that keen on it practically. It seems to me God the Creator plus Cindy the artist equals two, which makes all of my endeavors collaborative efforts, right? Truly now, must I involve everyone else? They can be so difficult and annoying and … did I mention annoying?

Author Barry Krammes once said, "Working together collaboratively is messy business, but outcomes often exceed initial expectations. Furthermore, collaboration helps us understand our own discipline better. It often leads to developments within our area of expertise that would have been impossible without working together."[1]

Krammes' statement is loaded with truth. Collaborating is messy. But equally true is that collaborating does make me a better artist. A better leader. A better person. And a better Christ-follower. It has taken me years to admit it, but I am a far better "we" than I am a "me."

Can I give you one final picture of the power of collaboration, just to prove out Paul's point that fluid unity is better than solo stints any day of the week?

Our worship leader and I were sitting in my office one day, trying to come up with a creative element for an upcoming Easter service. (Extra points for collaboration, no?) We were listening to the lyrics of a song we really wanted to do with our choir when the thought hit me: "What if we brought the words of the song to life in the form of a painting—a painting that would be painted onstage while the song was being sung?"

"That's it!" he cheered.

I picked up the phone to see if one of our most talented artists would be interested. I played the song for her over the phone, waiting anxiously for it to finish so I could get her thoughts on our idea. As she gave us her "Yes," another thought crossed my mind.

"Rita, what if, in addition to you, we had two other artists onstage … and all three of you painted on the same canvas?"

The first rehearsal rolled around, and the three painters took their places. Our band and choir began the song, and three hands reached for three brushes. Their first attempt came in at seven and a half minutes, which was two minutes too long. Each artist talked about what needed to be done differently, and then they tried it again. And again. And again.

Finally, they nailed it. Five minutes, twenty-eight seconds. Whew.

Earlier in the week, though, things hadn't been quite so easy. One artist didn't like another's choice of crimson for the tomb. Another felt sure that his colleague's representation of Jesus' face was simply too abstract for the painting's overall vibe. And then there was the issue of standing in each other's light. If memory serves, those first few meetings ended with everyone's nerves a little on the raw side.

Easter is always a special weekend because of how many spiritual investigators it attracts. But that particular year was extra special. In the end, six services yielded six works of art, paintings that reflected the miraculous story of Jesus' death, burial, and resurrection in warm red, orange, and gold. The cross, the crown of thorns, the empty tomb. Each time, as the last words were sung, the word "Finished" was painted in red in the right-hand corner of the canvas. And each time, an entire congregation rose to their feet to thank the God who was willing to see His own Son killed in order to kill sin for good in our lives.

Worshippers wiped their tears, raised their hands, shouted their thank-yous, and smiled knowing smiles at the truth of that word. Finished. Death is finished. Sin is finished. Hopelessness is finished. Because of what Christ did on the cross, all unrighteousness could once and for all be declared, "Finished."

Painful process? At times, certainly. Messy? You can bet your life on it. But what a glorious end result it is when creation honors Creator by choosing the course He Himself chose, the course of collaboration.

I said no to Nashville today. And it was largely due to this powerful collaboration with the team—*my* team—that caused me to do so. I'm committed to loving my team with a fresh sense of urgency. I'm committed to pouring into them and rooting for them and hopefully leading them well. And, unless a new offer surfaces that involves daily massages and complimentary miniature-umbrella-boasting drinks on a wireless-access-capable beach, I think I'll be doing this, here, with them, for a long, long time.

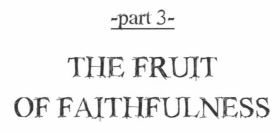

-part 3-

THE FRUIT
OF FAITHFULNESS

-7-
GUARDING THE DEPOSIT

Leader to Leader: How to Lead Well

Artists are not easy to lead, and artists desperately need leadership.
—Nancy Beach
Executive Vice President for the Arts,
Willow Creek Association

Guard this precious thing placed in your custody by the Holy Spirit.
—2 Timothy 1:14 MSG

ALTHOUGH MANY PEOPLE wrestle and strive and strain their way into leadership positions, I sort of fell into mine. I'd gone on staff at a local church in what we now call the worship-arts department, and mere months after my full-time arrival, the worship pastor (and my boss) decided to take a few months off.

He'd been on staff for seven years and—the nerve of him—he thought he finally deserved a break. On an otherwise peaceful Tuesday morning, I got called into his office, informed of his decision, and handed a baton I wasn't altogether sure I wanted to run with. "Would you be interested in leading while I'm away?" he asked.

In response to his question, I gave my best "Don't I look incredibly calm for someone who's just been thrust into a raging anxiety attack?" look. "Are you out of your mind?" I said out loud.

He said that he wasn't.

> "I'm still learning how to be an artist. Now you want me to lead a bunch of them?" Obviously, he and I had differing definitions of what constituted one being out of one's mind. Regardless, I was about to get a crash course in the importance of caring, serving, and leading well.

KEEP THE ARTISTS

Over the years, I've heard pastors and other leaders say they don't have the time or the energy to invest in artists. They don't understand them, or maybe they just don't *want* to understand them. Some leaders think they'll lose control, as though artists are plotting to take over the world. Others are scared of what the artists will dream up. What if their ideas are too far outside the box? What on earth would we do then?

> True, it's not easy to merge left-brain leaders and right-brain creatives.
> On the rare occasion when it does happen,
> angels are probably deployed from heaven to preside
> over the miracle that has just occurred.

But despite the challenges involved in leading artists, excluding them from the game altogether is simply not an option. Try though I may, I haven't been able to find any verses in the Bible that direct leaders to build the kingdom of God leveraging everyone but the artists in their midst. Good, bad, or otherwise, I think we've got to keep the artists.

Recently, I had the privilege of participating in a roundtable discussion with a dozen or so pastors and artists. The conversation migrated to what we as a collective group thought leaders of artists needed to do in order to be effective. Ideas from every direction started popping like corn kernels in a microwave, every participant offering their best thinking on how to lead the sometimes wacky, often emotional group known as artists. *If we must keep our artists,* the thinking went, *then how can we learn to work with them better?*

I did my best to pay attention to everyone's comments, but I was a bit distracted by the stream of insight God was pouring into my mind and heart. I jotted down the thoughts as quickly as they came to me and spent weeks afterward just ruminating on them.

What emerged from that time of reflection was a short list of "deposits" that leaders must make in the lives of the artists they lead. I've always loved the verse that says we should guard the "good deposit that was entrusted to you—guard it with the help of the Holy Spirit" (2 Tim. 1:14), and it's as if God was saying to me through my new list, "Cindy, I've made countless deposits in your life, including a pretty big one called leadership. Now, I'm asking you to make deposits in the lives of the ones you lead."

The rest of this chapter is devoted to the divine deposits I captured that day. There are six of them, and they are the culmination of what I've learned—often the hard way—since that morning in my boss's office when I became a freshly appointed Leader of Artists. Whether you are responsible for artists who are on staff, who fill volunteer teams, or who are presently doing nothing more than taking up pew space on Sunday mornings, just waiting to be asked to participate, I hope that as you read these ideas, you'll start taking seriously your role to guard the deposits God has entrusted to you.

DEPOSIT #1: ACCEPTANCE

For centuries now, artists in the local church have been sorely missed, both in terms of their presence and their production. On any given Sunday, hundreds of thousands of them are sitting in the pews of every local church on the planet, underappreciated and uninvited to come use their gifts for God's glory. If we don't extend this simple yet powerful invitation to them to get into the game, then there they'll sit till the sun goes down.

> In local churches large and small, artists
> must be accepted by
> those who lead them. They need to be welcomed in.
> Moreover, they need to be welcomed home.

Our senior pastor frequently uses what I call "art language" when he teaches. He doesn't preach so much as he paints a picture of each point he hopes to convey. His sentences include such texture you swear you can reach out and touch them, and from my vantage point in the sound booth near the rear of the auditorium each weekend, I notice heads bobbing in understanding the entire time he talks.

On most weekends, following each worship service, my artist-friends stop by to show me their sermon notes. Rather than seeing filled-in blanks, I notice elaborate sketches all the way to paper's edge of each key point that was made. Our pastor faithfully and intentionally captivates the artistic mind during his teaching time, and it's a gesture that is *never* lost on believer-artists in our midst. Finally, they are acknowledged and accepted. Finally, they have a place to belong.

Good leaders love and embrace the artists in their midst. Instead of shying away, they grant them *wild* acceptance. They spend time with them. They get to know them. They carve out an hour to meet with a group of them at a local coffee shop and listen to their dreams. They study how their creative minds work and ask questions about how the creative process unfolds. They invite them into their boardroom and their living room alike, because they value them as real (not to mention, God-given) companions.

Whether these leaders really "get" art or not, they accept artists' perspectives and points of view, their interpretations and insights. They are open to being stretched in their own way of thinking and gladly make the deposit of acceptance into artists' lives.

If you're in a leadership position, consider when you last spent intentional time with an artist or artist group. If it's been a while, call them today and set something up. Learn about their passions, about their current projects, and about what energizes them, what makes them feel honored, and what words of encouragement keep their spirits buoyed. Above all, listen well.

DEPOSIT #2: CHALLENGE

About a year ago, I realized that our visual artists were in a rut. For a long stretch of time, we'd been hanging the same type of art in our hallway gallery, show after show after show. Things finally became so stale and stagnant that I knew I had to take action.

Our church's visual-arts group I mentioned previously meets one Saturday morning a month in order to brainstorm upcoming events and arts shows, as well as to practice our crafts as artists. One of these meetings was coming up, and suddenly, I had an idea for how to dislodge the group from their rut.

I arrived at our meeting spot early and got busy flipping off overhead lights and draping the little window that let in light from outside. The team arrived, person by person, wondering why we were all sitting silently in a pitch-black room.

I opened with prayer and posed one simple question. "How does it feel in here?"

The answers were short and sarcastic at first: "Uh, dark?"

"Like someone forgot to pay the electric bill?"

"Like I could've stayed in bed."

Once the wisecracks were out of the way, though, more substantive answers emerged.

"It feels ... cold. And empty. Bleak."

"I can't see anyone's eyes ... there's no point of connection anywhere."

"I feel blinded. Unsure of what I'm doing here, which way I'm facing, and who's around me."

Over the next twenty minutes or so, I lighted candles, one taper at a time. The artists continued to share what changes they were seeing and how it was making them feel. They drew parallels to the spiritual journey and what it must be like for a human soul to suddenly find light. I asked them to capture their key words on a large piece of paper, which eventually would help many of them to create beautiful, original, passionate pieces of artwork. Rut-free art, you might say. We called the show that materialized "Illumination."

Kathleen, one of the visual artists, recently told me how much she needed our visual-arts community. When I probed the reasons why, she said, "It's too easy to stay in one area and not allow myself to think or act outside of those boundaries."

With the help of our brainstorming sessions, though, she'd stepped across the line, entering an entirely new arena of creativity. She was being challenged, which was leading to increased obedience to create. Not to mention better art.

Leaders of artists must challenge their artists to create—
consistently, effectively, and from a place of passion.

If you are not equipped to challenge the artists you lead in these ways, then lean into someone who is. Have your team read an inspiring book together, or bring in a speaker or a facilitator who knows what it's like to be stuck in the mud, creatively speaking, and then take good notes as you watch them go to work on your team.

DEPOSIT #3: CLARITY

Although most artists patently hate deadlines, *honest* artists admit that they really do need them. Artists I know can be told two months out about a deadline and still will be found tweaking paint or rewriting the chorus the night before it's due. Art is never "good enough" for the artist. As the leader, you've got to give them a cutoff point, as well as clear expectations regarding how to get from where they are to wherever you're asking them to go.

A few years back, our worship-arts team decided to produce an original musical written by a very talented member of our church. Hundreds of hours had been invested in crafting the script and the score, and since it was a brand-new production, we needed a brand-new set to complement it. An incredible designer in our church was asked to oversee the entire process on a volunteer basis, and as the set began to take shape, we all knew we'd tapped the right guy. But as opening night neared, I noticed that his fantastic attention to detail was going to cause the paint job to take three weeks longer than we had planned. Suffice it to say, we didn't have three extra weeks.

When the drama director and I met to discuss the dilemma, we decided the best course of action was to keep reminding him of the deadline we had established and of the expectations we had set, details that often fall out of artists' brains when they're hip deep in creation mode.

Invite your artists "in."
Give them a real challenge.
But then be sure to provide clear direction
and the right amount of
time to rehearse the song or produce
the video or paint the set so that
they can feel the thrill of successfully
contributing to the overall cause.

To do otherwise is to demonstrate something south of *excellence*, both in terms of your leadership and their finished product. In those situations, nobody wins. You lose, because the end result is less than you had hoped it would be. And your artists lose, because they walk away believing they have disappointed not only you, but God.

Can I give you one more note on this subject of setting clear expectations for your artists? Keep in mind that they are not typically nine-to-five people. It's true for me, and it's true for many of the artists in your midst.

Sometimes, early morning hours lend themselves to bursts of

creative insight. Other times, the moment I begin to drift off to sleep (usually on the couch, usually with laptop perched on my midsection), a wild hit of inspiration comes, and I'm immediately up and running. As leaders, we'd all do well to remember that artists aren't always capable of flipping the creative switch and producing fantastic results. Give your artists time and space, and not only will you see better things produced, but you'll also notice a saner process unfolding along the way.

DEPOSIT #4: ENCOURAGEMENT

The right words conveyed at the right time can
be the difference between an artist staying the
course on their artistic journey
and ditching their endeavor altogether.

Your artists need to believe that you "get" them. They need to know you're standing in their corner. And they need to hear you cheering them on, whether they're attempting to write a poem, considering auditioning for a role in an upcoming performance downtown, or touching brush to canvas for the very first time.

I was hanging out with my team during a new art show intake when one of our newer artists walked through the doors of our church auditorium. There, pressed against her chest with arms shielding each side, were two pieces of artwork. You would have thought she was carrying a newborn baby for the clenched grip she had on those frames.

When she didn't immediately set them down, I knew something

was wrong. I saw lines of tension form on her forehead and gently pulled her away from the team to ask what was the matter. She told me that this was her very first show and admitted feeling quite nervous about allowing anyone to see her work.

I coaxed her, one sentence at a time, into handing over the pieces, and I noticed strains of fear and worry dissipating once she'd let go. The paintings were beautiful, and I told her so. But that was hardly the point of our exchange. What I loved in the brief moments we shared was that, as a leader, I was able to help her trade in stress for a sparkle in her eye that made her whole face light up. A "You can do it" or "It's okay to let go" is sometimes all it takes, but what a profound deposit we make when you and I utter words like these!

DEPOSIT #5: TRUTH

One Sunday morning during rehearsal, I noticed our worship leader behaving a bit strangely. He was leading from our satellite location eight miles across town, but even via the image magnification screen I was watching him on, I could tell he wasn't his usual warm, engaging self. When the rehearsal was finished, I reached for my cell phone and called him at the other campus.

"Hey … is everything okay over there?"

"Yeah," he said, "things are fine."

We both knew that wasn't the truth. I pressed him further, calmly but persistently asking a few follow-up questions. Finally, he admitted that he'd overheard someone making a negative comment about his worship leading a couple of weeks prior and hadn't quite gotten over the sting of the moment. I was the first person he'd told.

Now, as he was trying to lead a rehearsal, little voices were running around in his head, cackling criticisms at him left and right.

Trusting the Spirit to guide, I said, "Dan, do you trust me?"

He said he did.

I began to speak truth to Dan about who God had called him to be and what role he was being asked to play that morning. I pointed out that he had been listening to the wrong voices ever since he'd overheard the critical remarks about his leadership capabilities, and that he was allowing Satan a powerful victory by letting those voices drown out the still, small voice of God.

The conversation brought Dan out of his funk just long enough to allow him to hear the truth. I prayed for him, and we ended the call. Later, when the service was under way, I marveled over the fact that Dan's mind and heart had embraced truth, and the result was a powerful time of worship for all of us.

Another situation required my telling the truth to a chronically late drummer. I'd watched him for several weeks as he arrived to a six-thirty rehearsal at ten till seven or seven fifteen. I approached him privately to make sure he was indeed aware of our agreed-upon start time. He openly admitted to the problematic pattern and promised to get his act together by the following week.

I told him I thought this was a very good idea.

Pointing out a flaw in an artist's attitude or action is never fun or easy, but Ephesians 4:15 (NLT) says that it's only by "speaking the truth in love" that we will in all things grow up into Christ.

You and I both know that truth-telling conversations don't always go well, but when your artists know your input comes from a heart full of love for God and for them, they'll listen closely to all that you have to say. Then the choice is up to them.

DEPOSIT #6: YOUR BEST YOU

As leaders, we can accept artists and challenge them, encourage them and tell them the truth, and yet we're absolutely no good to anyone if we're not taking care of our own souls. After years of stubbing my toe on this reality, I have finally come to grips with the fact that as a leader, doing "God's work" does not give me license to neglect my own soul care.

I've had to learn to pay attention to the
dashboard of my life and realize that when the tank is empty, it's
really empty.
You cannot give what you don't have.

I also cannot neglect the needs of my family. I had a revelation two years ago that just about leveled me. I had distanced myself from my family, all of whom live in Missouri. The realization finally hit me that I didn't even care if we talked on a consistent basis. I had put those relationships on the back burner and turned the heat way, way down.

Slowly, (*very* slowly), they allowed me back into the details of their lives. It was an awkward and sometimes painful process, but after several months of weekly phone and e-mail conversations, my mom once again knew I was available to hear about the latest family news, my dad knew I wanted the details on that week's fishing catch, and my nieces and nephew knew they had an Aunt Cindy who loved them and who cared about the ins and outs of their young lives. These days, experiencing Jocie's paintings, Matthew's ball games, and Lauren's dance recitals—even if virtually, through DVDs and digital photos—is one of the most precious parts of my week. When I consider all that I missed during my several-year absence, it makes me cringe.

A third area that I simply cannot neglect is my relationship with God. When I bypass God on a regular basis and run on my own jet fuel instead of looking to Him for strength, I am prone to making decisions that lead my team down the wrong path. The danger of getting into a weekly rhythm of planning and executing without any Spirit-led guidance is that I fall into outright disobedience at worst, and missed moments when God could have used me to have an impact in others' lives at best.

Sure, there are days when I make mistakes and feel as though the sky is falling. Doubts and fears creep in, and I am tired and lonely. But it is in those moments that God reminds me He is big enough to carry it all. A strong sense of security shows up when I recall that He is the Leader, and I simply must *follow*. "I am the LORD," God promises in Exodus. "I will bring you out from under the yoke.... I will free you.... I will redeem you.... I will take you.... I will be your God.... I am the LORD your God.... I will bring you to the land.... I will give it to you.... I am the LORD" (Ex. 6:6–8).

God is the One who will do the work. And when I regain the perspective that says God has every leadership issue solved, every personnel matter handled, every weekend service planned, every question already answered, I feel His calm, reassuring peace wash over me once more. It is in *His* supernatural strength that *I* can do all things. What a relief!

Moses understood this idea well: In the depths of his heart, he knew that without God, he would fumble and nothing would ever be accomplished. In Exodus 33:15 (MSG), he says, "If your presence doesn't take the lead here, call this trip off right now. How else will it be known that you're with me in this, with me and your people?"

When *that* is the cry of our heart as leaders, a lot of things fall into place. Using the tabernacle-building project as an example, let me give you three by-products Moses experienced as a result of his God-centered heartbeat.

Show Up

Moses refused to isolate himself from God or from the artists he led. Moses didn't just check out and take a vacation while the tabernacle was finished and set up. Instead, he showed up. Exodus 39:32–42 says that once all the work on the tabernacle was completed, the artists took it to Moses, who inspected it from every angle to make sure it meshed with the original blueprint. After all, he was the only one who had seen the prototype. He examined the loops of blue material. He counted gold clasps until they numbered fifty. He checked and double-checked all eleven curtains, running his makeshift ruler along each one until he was certain they were thirty cubits long and four cubits wide. He counted the forty silver bases. Tested the gold crossbars. Located the ark made of acacia wood. He inspected every seam, measured the placement of every stone, and revisited every wooden frame to ensure it was positioned just so. By scrutinizing every last detail "as the LORD commanded," he proved just how much skin he had in the game.

Imagine how strong and creative worship services would be if every leader grasped this concept! Pastors would work arm in arm with worship leaders and arts teams to make a difference not only in our churches and community but all over the earth. (Are you humming Louie Armstrong's "What a Wonderful World" too?)

Moses knew he had a specific role to play and didn't try to delegate it to anyone else. He didn't cast vision for this project and then take a sabbatical. He stayed on course through the good times and the not-so-good times alike, taking responsibility for leading his artists instead of treating his role as a separate and disjointed effort.

Leaders cannot afford to isolate themselves from those they lead.

Just in case you blinked, I'll say it again. Leader, you cannot afford to isolate yourself from those you lead. To do so is to leave a team perilously close to sanity's edge as they question your authority and your ability to lead. Behave this way long enough, and you will lose their respect and their trust altogether. At every turn, your team will wonder if you're on the verge of a nervous breakdown or perhaps about to quit. Truly, absence does not always make the heart grow fonder. You simply must show up—mind, body, heart, and soul.

Let Go

In my early years of leading, I was a bit of a control freak. I wanted everything to be perfect, and since nobody seemed to prize my standard as I did, I had to do everything myself. I released zero responsibilities to my team, and as a result, I sank under the burden of the heavy load I insisted on carrying. I was exhausted, projects fell apart, and nobody wanted to be around me anymore (go figure).

Needless to say, my mode of operation was a far cry from how Moses chose to lead. Exodus 36 schools me every time I read it: It says that Moses released resources to his team of artists and then *released his artists* to go do the work. *They* made the curtains. *They* made the clasps. *They* made the tent covering. *They* made the acacia wood frames. In short, Moses let go, which I had never seemed to be able to do.

Inviting those around us to join in the creative process always produces something better than what we could produce alone. (Two are better than one, anyone?) Give your artists the tools they need, stand with them while they're learning whatever task they've been given, and be willing to let them give it a whirl on their own.

Bless Freely

Exodus 39:43 says that Moses "saw that they had done it *just as the LORD had commanded*," and so he blessed them. Moses blessed his artists freely, both for their obedience to God for doing the work in the first place, and for their attention to detail in doing the work well. Artists are dying for this level of input!

As Moses put the finishing touches on the tabernacle and the glory of God filled it, I envision a sense of awe overwhelming the hearts of all those who had contributed their skilled labor to the task. The job was finally complete! The work to which God had called them was now finished, and in exchange they received His *blessing*, courtesy of their faithful leader. What a gift!

It's one of leadership's greatest perks,
this ability we have to bless our teams on behalf of God.

As you bless your artists, be specific with your input. Force yourself to express why a certain lyrical line calls you into worship or why a particular detail in a painting caught your attention. And watch your body language as you do it: Your tone, your facial expressions, your posture—these things often speak louder to the heart of an artist than even the words coming from your lips. "Great job" may be a meaningful phrase to you, but artists crave specific validation and acknowledgment that helps them make sense of their God-given talent. Tell them why their art matters, to God, to other worshippers, and to you. Bless your artists freely, leader. The role is yours and yours alone.

WORTH IT ALL

If we're honest with each other, dealing with people who aren't always open to input, who dodge deadlines, who are typically late, who desire to work on their own, and who often cop the attitude of a roller coaster having a very bad day doesn't sound all that appealing. (Which is why, on more than one occasion, I have dreamed of applying to become a greeter at my local Wal-Mart, itchy blue Here to Help vest and all.)

But for the past decade, I've seen God use the gifts of faithful artists to melt cold hearts and transform lukewarm lives. Second glances have been cast toward art hanging in our church's hallway gallery. Ears have perked up to take in well-delivered lines from an actor onstage. Eyes have glistened with tears as on-screen Scriptures come to colorful, animated life.

For all of their idiosyncrasies, there isn't another group of people on the face of this planet that I'd rather be associated with than artists. They move me, touch me, stretch me, and hold me accountable to practice my own art form. They have stood in front of me, walked behind me, and knelt beside me when I've walked through difficult seasons of ministry. To abdicate my role in working with and leading artists would be to turn them away to a world that cannot offer them hope or purpose for their art, save earning a few bucks from an art sale or receiving a round of applause for a song well sung.

You and I have been challenged to guard the deposit God has asked for us to steward so that, with His guidance and strength, truth and beauty can get ushered into this fallen world through various forms of art. Our diligent efforts as leaders help the kingdom of God to expand and thrive. It is *this* knowledge that makes it all worth it.

Think of a recent ministry event or ministry season
you were responsible for leading. Based on the
six criteria below, how well did you do at leading
the artists you oversaw? Rate yourself on all six
"deposits" and then consider which one or two might
serve as growth areas for you going forward.

- Acceptance
- Challenge
- Clarity
- Encouragement
- Truth
- Your "Best You"

-8-

YOU ARE HERE

Providing Platforms for the Artists You See

*In order to communicate the message entrusted to us
by Christ, the Church needs art.
Art has a unique capacity to take one or another facet
of the message and translate it into
colors, shapes, and sounds that nourish the intuition
of those who look or listen.*[1]
—POPE JOHN PAUL II

I WAS ON the road recently and with an hour of downtime before my next meeting decided to indulge in a little retail therapy at the mall across the street from my hotel. I'd never been there before, so I actually paid attention to where I parked (shocking, really) and which entrance I used so I could make it back out without any trouble.

I was a kid in a candy store, buzzing in and out of a dozen new-to-me shops and quaint boutiques. My weighted-down forearm proved just how much fun power-shopping can be, but lugging around all those bags can make a girl hungry. I headed for the food court to find some semblance of protein, and that's when it hit me. In my enthusiastic frenzy, I'd covered three quadrants and four levels of the mall and now had no idea how to get back to my starting point.

Sixty seconds later, I was standing in front of the map-of-the-mall display. As soon as I found the yellow arrow that said "You Are Here," a dose of relief coursed through my veins. What a smart sign! Down two flights of stairs and past three of my now-favorite stores, and *voila*! I located the door that led me right to my car.

What on earth does this have to do with leading artists, you ask?

Years ago, one of the biggest mistakes I made in my leadership role was performing an inadequate and unrealistic assessment of where we as a group really "were." I saw the paths that other, larger, more resourced churches were taking and coveted their capability for ushering in artistic excellence in their setting. Why couldn't we look like them, sound like them, and do what they were doing? Why couldn't *we* be where *they* were? Well, it turns out, because we *weren't* where they were.

A real danger for churches today—my own church included—
is in believing that our arts communities should
look like everyone else's arts community.

We think that we're "here" when really we're over "there." And the misalignment can be terribly detrimental to an arts community's health. To get where I wanted to go in the mall that day, I had to first get clear on where I really was. It's a practice that works in other environments as well, including that of the local church.

When I first started in ministry, our church had a whole bunch of musicians, vocalists, and actors but was pretty light on dancers, writers, and visual artists. Interestingly, instead of fully leveraging the artists who were right in front of me, I poured myself into trying to find platforms for every art form under the sun. Truly, I thought that in order to embrace the arts, we had to embrace *all* the arts, whether we had artists from those disciplines in our church or not.

Here's the reality: Not every church will have every kind of medium represented in their congregation. What's more, there may be seasons during which one art form is employed more than others. If you are a leader of artists, do yourself a huge favor: Let this reality be okay! In other words, if you're feeling pressure to be like your neighbor down the road, slow down and remember that you serve the Creator of creativity Himself who has a bigger vision for you than the cookie-cutter dreams you're dreaming.

To discover where your church's particular "You Are Here" arrow is pointing, ask:

What is God calling us to do, in our church? Sure, attending conferences and visiting other churches is inspiring, but what is God's plan for *our* distinct body of believers?

What does God seem to be saying to me as the leader or champion of the arts at this church?

Will I be obedient to that calling?

What kinds of artists are standing right in front of me? What existing talent can I leverage right now? If the actors in my midst can't deliver a line without choking, then maybe God's not calling us to have a drama ministry right this minute. If nobody in our church can string six paragraphs together into a compelling and interesting story, then maybe a dedicated writers' ministry isn't a platform we need to invest in just yet.

During the last decade, the church at large
has experienced massive
growth and innovation in everything from
technology and design
to creativity and community.

We've married the old with the new. Cathedrals have evolved into café-gymnatoriums. Altars are now stair-encrusted theatrical stages. Traditional hymns have morphed into contemporary worship songs. Hymnbooks themselves have been replaced by projected images via concert-scale video systems. Music Directors have slid into the role of full-fledged Worship Leaders. Sunday-school rooms have been supplanted with bookstores and coffee bars. Single church dwellings have reproduced to form multisite campuses.

Enter, the artist!

The time is now to establish platforms or intentional opportunities for artists to exercise their gifts and help people engage with God. And truly, the sky is the limit on how to get that done!

As you read of the three primary platforms our church has established in order to free up artists in our midst—the weekend worship service, creation of an intentional visual-arts community, and establishment of an intentional technical arts community—let them spur you on to establish healthy and appropriate platforms that adequately reflect where *you* are as a church.

PLATFORM #1: WEEKEND WORSHIP SERVICES

Every weekend, in churches in every city in the world, thousands of men, women, and children step into sanctuaries and theaters and worship centers, each and every one of them representing a significant and unique journey. Many are looking to deepen their relationship with Christ. Some are seeking answers. Still others need to be talked down from their ledges … and fast!

As staff members and volunteers, as artists, as fellow sojourners, we are challenged to create authentic worship experiences where hope, grace, and God's redeeming love can be experienced. It's a hefty weight to bear, but one the role of the artist can lessen.

Each art medium can be powerful by itself, but my experience proves that when the arts are layered—such as when a drama is followed by a moving song, or when an artist completes a painting onstage during a reflective worship set, or when dramatic lighting outlines a dancer's silhouette during her final pose—God sneaks even further into the congregation's collective soul.

Artists communicate truth through their original art,
and truth is what knocks down walls of
defense surrounding the human heart
and elicits marvelous, glorious life change.

Like most ministries today, our church relies on the talents of musicians, singers, and worship leaders every single weekend during the all-familiar "weekend worship experience." And it's great! But increasingly over the last ten years, we have expanded our thinking here. The band has swelled to include nontraditional instrumentalists such as violinists, mandolin players, harmonica players, and trumpet players. We've incorporated the mediums of dance, drama, painting, and sculpting into our services. And in doing so, we've provided a fantastic, God-honoring avenue for artists who would have never thought they could use their gifts in a local church, let alone touch thousands of lives, to do just that.

You don't get this level of quality and impact, though, unless your church has done some due diligence on the front end. Over the past several years, our staff team and senior pastor have hashed through three strategic elements that allow our artists to contribute in predictably meaningful ways today. Those elements include development of a worship philosophy, setting of high standards, and the ongoing practice of beginning with the end in mind.

Develop a Worship Philosophy

The day our team committed our worship philosophy to print was a marvelous day. Finally, everyone could get on the same page regarding our intentions and expectations pertaining to worship! Finally, we'd have a grid to determine how we make decisions and accomplish our mission. Talk about a great accountability tool!

Having a formalized philosophy forces our entire team—
staff and volunteers alike—to maintain
laserlike focus as we pray
and plan and execute each and every programming element.

If your worship-arts community does not have a worship philosophy,

consider coming up with one. Read the one that follows, asking the
Spirit to point out key words to help you get started in structuring your
own version.

Woodmen Valley Chapel
Philosophy of Worship

We operate from a posture of amazement: amazement
over the reality that God is really enough; amazement
over what He has done for us through Jesus Christ; and
amazement over His kingdom purposes to which we have
been called. Each stitch of our story is laced together
with amazement, with wonder, and with worship.

God
Ultimately, worship is not about us.
God summons all of His creation to acknowledge and
engage with His worth. For each of us, our view of God
is the axis on which the rest of our lives turn. A high
view of God, therefore, dictates a vibrant cadence of
worship.

Life
Worship means honoring God for who He is and for
what He is up to in our lives. "Lifestyle" worship involves
submitting to Him at every bend in the road, whether the
stage of our journey is marked by brokenness or beauty,
by laughter or by tears.

Authenticity

In Isaiah 29:13, Jesus warns against worshipping apart from an engaged heart. Disengagement stems from outright rebellion against God because of sin, but it also occurs when our hearts are apathetic or disinterested in spiritual things. Relevance in corporate worship settings elicits authentic worship from participants.

Substance

Relevance, while important, will not equate to sacrifices on the substance front. Indeed, the more substantive are our lives, continuously to deepen our biblical and theological moorings by acknowledging the historicity of our faith, the more relevant we become.

Witness

Evangelism occurs in the context of God-centered worship, whether that worship exists on a personal or a corporate level. As we provide interesting and accurate expressions of God's character, beauty, and grace for those not yet persuaded by the gospel, we bear witness to the core of the Christian life.

Community

The goal of corporate worship is to engage a community of God's people in a corporate exaltation of His wonder and authority. Worship leaders, then, are facilitators of communal celebration honoring one and only one Guest of honor, God Himself.

Arts

The practice of corporate worship allows for the excellent execution of multiple art forms—not just music—to play a role. All art forms are welcomed to help worshippers process God's truth and mystery. From paint to film, from dance to drama, from the technical to the visual, excellent worship elicits meaningful engagement from every facet of creativity, as ordained and encouraged by the Creator Himself.

Creativity

The worship of God as Creator is central to the heart of His creation. All that we do in the context of corporate worship—praying prayers, taking risks, singing songs, practicing art—is born of the desire to celebrate His creativity as a worshipping community.

Set a Standard of Excellence

Establishing your overall worship philosophy is a critical step to take. But keep in mind that it's just words on a page unless you enforce a standard of excellence that upholds it.

Somewhere along the way, I discovered that it is unfair to ask the congregation to tolerate a creative standard that is vastly lower than what they're exposed to all week long as they hear exquisitely produced music from their car's CD player, witness well-structured scenes and beautifully designed sets on movie theater screens, and enjoy the incredible attention to ambiance paid by a local dining establishment. Whether they want to or not, churchgoers step into churches each weekend with a preset expectation of excellence. If we want to hold their enthusiasm, then our artists must create *quality* art.

Now, if you're the leader of all those artists, I know what you're probably thinking: *What do I do with Mildred?*

"Mildreds" love to sing onstage on Sunday morning but sadly can't carry a tune in a bucket. They exist in every church. And most often, they're indulged because they have been so faithful for so many years that to oust them from the worship team would surely mean our own ousting from heaven itself. So, out of sheer obligation, we overlook their pitch problems and ignore the congregation-wide squirming that ensues every time they take the stage. Which all would be just fine, except for the fact that this dynamic is honoring neither to God nor to any Mildred I've ever known.

God asks for our very best worship. True, it's easy to become mechanical and focus more on getting enough warm bodies onstage than on the real heart behind why we do what we do. But God detests this approach! "These people come near to me with their mouth and honor me with their lips, but their hearts are far from me," God said through the prophet Isaiah. "Their worship of me is made up only of rules taught by men" (Isa. 29:13).

I don't know about you, but I do not want to be numbered among the hearts-far-from-God group.

So, we do our best to be prepared, mind, soul, heart, and spirit. And then we pass on that expectation to those we lead. "If the worship leader asks you to be on time," we say, "then arrive ten minutes early. It won't kill you, really." Or, "If the charts and digital files have been posted on the Web for four days, then there's really no excuse for showing up unrehearsed." Or, "If the Spirit prompts us to switch out a song, please be flexible and submit with us to his leading."

> Subscribe to 2 Chronicles 29:11 (MSG), which says,
> "Children, don't drag your feet in this!
> GOD has chosen you to take your place
> before him to serve in
> conducting and leading worship—this is your
> life work;
> make sure you do it and do it well."

The fruit of our labor in this regard sounds something like this letter I received several weeks ago from a member of our congregation: "I could write for hours and still not fully express how much I appreciate those who lead and serve the body of Christ at Woodmen! In the four years that I've been attending here, I've never once sat through a service. Each weekend has catalyzed an encounter with the living God—an opportunity to worship Him, to fellowship with His people, and to be instructed in His Word regarding areas where I need to change. Your team's insistence on authenticity and excellence is always evident. I see your heart for God shine through in the 'big things' and in the million and one little things that support them. Thank you—all of you—for what you do." We must settle for nothing less than the very best from ourselves, and from our artists. Push them, challenge them, press them, and shake them. Do whatever you have to do, but refuse to let your team deliver less than their very, very best.

Begin with the End in Mind

A third aspect of due diligence that has served our artists well in the context of the weekend worship service is the practice of beginning with the end in mind, as it pertains to programmatic planning.

Here, give it a try: Put yourself in the shoes of someone walking through your church's doors on a Sunday morning. You've had a difficult week. Your spouse irritated you over breakfast. Your kids are unruly. Frankly, you're just hoping to sit quietly for an hour and have something get recalibrated in your mind and heart and soul so that next week won't be as completely abysmal as the one you've just completed.

Now, what's the first thing you see on the video screens? How about in the bulletin? Were you greeted with an encouraging smile and a warm handshake as you entered? What effect did the song set have on you? Was the teaching clear? Did the programmatic elements draw you in or turn you off?

If you are a producer or a worship leader, part of your role is to live the entire service before it happens. You must think through every single transition, whether verbal or musical. Are there places during the worship experience when everyone can slow down, take a breath, and allow the Spirit to move?

Read through each line of the lyrics of the worship song set. Is there celebratory energy at any point during the service? Does the drama set up the message, or are you performing it to show off your new actor? Is the new worship song really able to be sung by the congregation, or will they just sit there, waiting for the "professionals" to finish so they can move through the rest of the worship time?

Has Scripture been incorporated into the song set by
the leader or read out loud together as a group?
Artists do not participate
in worship services simply to entertain. Far from it!
Their task is to convey truth and to dispense hope.

Begin with the end in mind. And then invite each artist and member of the planning team to step backward into the creative elements that will best encourage, inspire, and motivate those who are attending.

PLATFORM #2: AN INTENTIONAL ARTIST COMMUNITY

In February 2000, along with a selected team of visual artists, we launched our second major artist platform—our church's visual-arts community, *imago Dei* (literally, "in God's image"). We ran an invitation in our church's bulletin, asking photographers, painters, sculptors, graphic designers, and any other fine artists to come to a Saturday-morning meeting. And more than two dozen of them showed. Which was good news, given I'd resigned myself to spending the morning alone, just my bag of bagels and me.

Many were pursuing their art as professionals, but others were just getting started. We spent a good portion of that first meeting simply exploring the question, What does it mean to be part of a visual-arts community within the context of a local church?

An early dream that cropped up among the group was to establish that hallway gallery leading into the church's worship center mentioned previously. Just in time for Mother's Day, we hosted our first exhibit, titled "New Life." The opening night reception included live musicians, a chef from a local hotel who was compelled to help us out, and ambiance to spare.

The door was officially swinging open for future visual artists in our church to step through.

Since that first gallery exhibit eight years ago, the hallway walls—officially, as of this year, "The Fireside Gallery at Woodmen Valley Chapel"—have had several thousand holes pounded into them as show after show was hung. (I'm sure our facilities team wonders if we realize just how much paint and spackle our department requires.) According to our city newspaper, we have officially become a "formal" gallery. But it all started with two dozen faithful folks who were ready to say yes to God.

If you are looking to start a visual-arts community in your setting, remember that starting small is better than not starting at all. Consider implementing one or two of the following practical ideas:

Place an ad in your church bulletin or on the church's Web site calling all fine artists to gather at an initial meeting. During that first meeting, find out what mediums are represented, as well as how often people are interested in meeting and what they hope to get out of your meetings.

Establish a small, volunteer-based leadership team, including someone to head up gallery shows, someone to head up artist receptions, and so forth.

Lay a solid foundation with these leaders by reading a book together, such as Rory Noland's *The Heart of the Artist*.[2]

Establish a consistent "gallery" in one hallway or another specially designated area of the building where you can rotate art every sixty or ninety days.

Host opening-night receptions with great food and live musicians.

Organize field trips, such as convening at a museum to take in the latest art exhibit.

Schedule workshops periodically to stretch and challenge each artist.

Whether you have three or twenty-three, stay committed to what God wants to do in and through their art.

One further consideration as it relates to establishing a visual-arts community is to keep in mind that even for the artist in the local church the be-all, end-all goal for us as Christ-followers is to accomplish the Great Commission.

Some time ago, God impressed me with a novel idea. We could use our church's gallery space not only to exhibit our *own* artists' work, but also the artwork of local artists in our community. A phone call to our local art guild later, and suddenly we had a hundred pieces of artwork hanging in our hallway gallery, most of it crafted by hands that had never once been raised in worship to God.

It has been three years now, and each time, that show takes the cake as the most eagerly anticipated one we do, by our artists and guild members alike.

PLATFORM #3: THE TECHNICAL ARTS

Ready for our church's third primary platform? As technology advances are made, more interesting and challenging opportunities emerge for the local church. To this point, one of the highlights of my ministry has been watching technicians establish their role as artists in executing the creative worship service.

Most join our ministry with pretty low expectations: They'll just run a camera or mess around on a computer; they'll just program a few lights or fiddle with knobs on a sound board. But then it happens. They catch sight of the fact that something far greater is going on. They "get" that they are a critical cog in the creativity wheel, and they're goners from that point on.

Wes is one of our lighting guys. At first, he volunteered one weekend a month. But now, he serves on a regular basis and arrives hours ahead of everyone else to change gels, focus lights, and establish the "feel" for each service. He paints with light, creating an unbelievable amount of dense color with a surprisingly limited number of light fixtures. Truly, with light and light alone, he leads a full house of worshippers into the presence of God. And he's teaching others to do the same. I received a note from Wes recently that said, "Thanks for allowing me to be part of this past weekend's services. The ability to bridge the gap between people and the glory of God is awesome. Many volunteers don't realize that we are part of a bigger picture. We are helping people enter into the kingdom of Heaven … for all of eternity. Have a great week! Wes."

Technical artists are hidden servants, seen only when something goes wrong. They stay up late, making sure lights are focused for upcoming productions, and arrive early to change batteries, test equipment, and ensure mics and other gear are in flawless, working order.

If you are in the early days of establishing an intentional technical arts community, perhaps a few pointers will save you from the
pitfalls I unwittingly visited. What follows are my top ten lessons
learned:

1. Make sure you have a competent technical team before you
purchase costly and complicated equipment. (Please read that sentence sixteen more times!)

2. As you grow, both in terms of personnel and equipment, make
sure your strategic plan reflects adequate maintenance, upgrades, and
implementation fees for installing new technology.

3. Develop an airtight training plan for each and every technical
position, regardless if the role is to be filled by staff or by volunteers. (Many of our best technicians had zero formal training before
they showed up but possessed immensely teachable spirits. Always
complement laudable attitudes with thorough training.)

4. Be diligent to build community. Chili cook-offs and flag foot-
ball games in the park go a long way in forging friendships among
team members.

5. Include technical artists in discussions pertaining to every arts
event you execute. This helps them see how they fit into the larger
worship-arts community.

6. Build a video production team, including those who plan on
the front end, shoot in the field, and edit during postproduction.

7. Continually remind technical artists of how crucial they are to
a weekend service. Often, attention is paid only to those onstage, but
the technical artist is just as important as all others when it comes
to enhancing worship leadership, especially with the proliferation of
multisite worship.

8. Find an advocate in leadership for releasing funds to purchase new equipment. For me, it's my boss, Doug. Every Tuesday, as part of our worship-planning meeting, he asks great questions like "What are the current needs?" "What needs to be purchased and why?" "How's maintenance on the existing gear?" He would not readily identify himself as an "artist type," but he sees immense value in the ability of the arts to accomplish kingdom goals in people's lives, and so he fights for resources for our department. What a gift!

9. Carefully evaluate every equipment purchase before you buy it; what's more, don't be afraid to rent a piece of gear first, in order to help senior leaders understand how the addition can benefit the overall vision of the church. The technical arts exist to enhance worship, not to distract congregants with unnecessary bells and whistles.

10. And, finally, *always* have food on hand. Technical artists will show up in greater quantity and with happier hearts when they know they will be fed.

FUTURE PLATFORMS

There are two future platforms that we are working on at our church. The first is something we call "NOW," which stands for Night of Worship. We've already executed the idea on a couple of occasions but continue to ask God how we might refine it for more consistent use. Essentially, NOW events are relatively unstructured opportunities for families to come together for a highly participatory worship experience.

The reason it serves as a fantastic platform is that there is no limit to how many artists and art forms you can incorporate. So, for example, if you walked into our worship center during a NOW experience, here's what you might see:

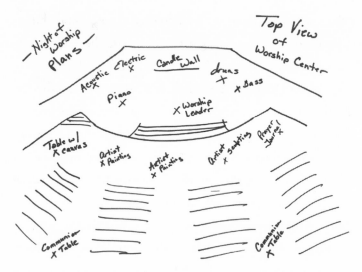

Station 1: Large, blank canvas and colored pens. No instructions. People express whatever they feel as they worship, which can result in a canvas full of images ranging from crosses to tears to outlines of children's hands, filled in with their parents' sentiments of gratitude to God.

Station 2: Communion elements. Worshippers approach the table at any time and participate in remembering what Christ did for humankind.

Station 3: Journal for those wishing to write down their thoughts or prayers.

Station 4: Visual art observation. Four artists were invited to create while the songs were being sung. People are invited to watch the artist and learn perhaps a different style of worship.

The first time we did this, the hour-and-a-half-long service was divided into two parts, with a break in between. Two different bands played, which allowed for more artists to share their gifts, and during the break, participants were invited to view artwork that had been set up in the guest center. Each piece had been donated to raise scholarship money for artists to attend an upcoming Artist Weekend. The result? More than a thousand dollars raised, which sent fifteen artists to the retreat.

Our first NOW experience drew more than four hundred participants, or a little less than 10 percent of our worshipping population. At the end of the evening, the blank canvas was filled with pictures and words of worship. The journal contained hundreds of entries, some crying out for God to save them, many expressing thanks for all God had done in their lives. What an honor it was to pray personally over those requests—each and every one—the following evening.

Most of the Communion elements were gone, and the majority of the artwork was sold. If God allows, our arts community will leverage this platform for years to come.

A second future platform that has not been tested in our church is the leveraging of our coffee bar as an intentional artist-friendly environment.

Over the last six months, I have received more invitations from artists who are making their debut in local coffee shops than ever before. Since it's rare today to walk into a church without detecting the aroma of coffee—ours included—why couldn't the church take the lead and offer this kind of platform for artists of all types, believer and nonbeliever, churchgoer and nonattendee alike?

One coffeehouse in California has an eighteen-month waiting list for artists who are anxious to display their artwork. A year and a half! So, with that in mind, my team and I have begun dreaming about the emergence of our own Friday-night coffeehouse. Artists would be invited to debut their latest CD, showcase their latest body of work, or read current essays they have written, all in a safe, nurturing environment. In addition to receiving real-time feedback, they'd also find community among others who "get" them.

As I say, we're still in the early stages of planning on this one. But the point is, we're anticipating future, God-given platforms that will serve to release the artists in our midst. Believing the words of Pope John Paul II, perhaps more than ever before, artists need the church, and the church needs artists! This is the backbone of the platform concept. Do your due diligence here, and you'll reap mind-blowing rewards. The details and specifics take some tending, but leading well and leaning on God's intervention in this regard makes for truly majestic moments in ministry. Perhaps the following chapter will give you a sense of what I'm talking about.

-9-

AN EMPTY ROOM FINDS ITS SOUL

One Leader's Experience One Weekend in May

Lord, make me see Thy glory in every place.
—MICHELANGELO

TRUE TO FORM for a Saturday, I have arrived early to tend to my chores before the team shows up. As I make my way up the stairs and through the hallway, arms loaded with extra copies of music charts, run sheets, bulletins, as well as three unopened bottles of water—*Got to stay hydrated, you know*—I can't help but smile as I scan dozens of artwork pieces hanging in our makeshift gallery. The sight stops me in my tracks. *Our best show yet. God-honoring. Passion-fueled. Amazing. Was the reception just last night? Man, the hours fly....*

Any evidence of the three hundred admirers who wandered our hallways to take in photographs and abstracts and paintings in watercolor and oil and acrylic has been dutifully removed, sometime between my late-night departure—well after ten o'clock, if memory serves—and now, just eleven hours later. In due time, worshippers will begin arriving for our evening service, and I know they'll join the ranks of the Officially Enamored who have been drawn in by the immensity and beauty of the artwork lining the entryway. I'll test my theory by paying attention to how many stragglers sneak into the service ten or fifteen minutes after the on-the-hour greeting has come and gone.

But all of this is not why I'm stuck indoors on a sunny-but-mild springtime Saturday morning.

I head toward the heavy wooden doors of the worship center, dig for my keys, and, finding them, slip the fat-headed one into the thick brass lock. The door whooshes shut behind me once I'm inside, and I gingerly step toward the sound booth, slim slivers of natural light peeking through the semiclosed blinds to guide my way. I pad my hand along the half-wall of the booth until my thumb detects the small, slick horizontal lever that will raise house lights all around me. Once a hint of illumination creeps in, I notice the dark wooden pews, the carpeted steps leading to the stage, the empty water bottles left from Thursday night's rehearsal. *Musicians—worse than messy, flighty schoolchildren.*

All is perfectly quiet, a reality not lost on me as I stand there wishing for the stillness to persuade my mind to slow down too. Somewhere along the way, it picked up the preposterous notion that its sole purpose in my Saturday experience was to whir and spin and tick off each item on my ever-lengthening Producer's Checklist in bold, blinking, neon fashion until I take notice. I indulge the nagging thoughts for fifteen seconds and run down my list of things to do, lying to myself in reassurances large and small that it's not that much, it won't take that long, things will all work out just fine. *Don't I wish.*

Funny, I walk through this routine every Saturday, and every Saturday, I hurriedly throw on the lights and crank up the music. All systems go. All senses stimulated. But for some reason today, I'm compelled to settle into the quiet a few beats longer. I let all that my arms have been carrying cascade onto the counter of the booth and collapse myself into a pew. When was the last time I simply sat … in silence … just to "be" with God?

I take two long, deep breaths, as if putting my mind on notice that this is what we're going to do for the time being. The list will have to wait.

My eyes drift across the room, back and forth, eventually fixing their gaze on the stage directly in front of me. The piano, drums, and keyboard are expressionless guards standing at attention, the monitors and microphones just as lifeless and cold. I think back to Thursday night's rehearsal with its penetrating vibe and sense of … anointing, actually, and telegraph to the gear onstage that there is no need to worry. Their music-making handlers will be arriving soon.

Thinking about those band members turns my lips smile-ward as I remember the start of that rehearsal and how it started like every other rehearsal we'd ever had. Still, after an entire decade—*ten long, sometimes ugly years*—I continue to struggle with their pervasive unwillingness to turn down their monitors for the sake of a decent house mix. The never-ending battle, but I know things could be far worse.

I close my eyes momentarily and envision the band and singers those few precious minutes after rehearsal had officially ended. Two years ago, we began a practice called "taking the pulse" in order to hear how every team member was doing before ending our time in prayer. A few artists who will serve tonight shared their heavy burdens with the group during that intimate, communal conversation forty-eight hours ago, and as I sit here now, I think about their aches and pains. I think about their pleas before God. I think about the stuff of life that knits us together. And I pray.

I pray for the team member who has just walked through a terrible divorce—is any divorce not terrible?—and is learning how to live life again, just her and her two children. Tonight will be her first time onstage after a several-month sabbatical—a time to heal, she hoped it would be.

I pray for another who divulged that he had been laid off recently from his job and is worried with meeting his family's most basic needs—groceries, a roof over their head, clothes on their backs. "God's direction regarding what to do next," he said, when I asked him how we could be praying. "And 'next,' you know, is sort of right now."

One of our vocalists said her daughter was going through a rebellious time. Anguish. Concern. Dismay. Hopelessness. Helplessness. Terrible nouns flooded her eyes, but all her lips said was, "I need wisdom. And patience. Please ask God to give me patience."

Each team member—each artist—human, through and through. Complete with the struggles and questions and heartaches humans have, not a single one exempt. This, despite congregation-people telling me week in, week out, how our vocalists, our sound technicians, our visual artists have it "so together." I tell them it isn't so, that to a person we are human beings, and frail ones, at that. "We have broken lives and broken dreams and broken spirits more times than we care to admit," I say.

But it's no use. Their perspectives are fixed, cement that only gets harder, not softer, with time.

This morning, as if needing to prove the fallibility-argument to myself, I replay last weekend's postservice reality, when a migraine so overtook my body that all I craved was my fluffy down pillow and a mysterious absence of humankind for a fifty-foot radius, at least. God and church and worshippers of all walks of life would have to go on without me. My time was up, my number was being called, and this particular headache was sure to do me in.

Thank You, God, I think on this side of the headache. *Ah, Your Spirit. Thank You for Your Spirit, who nudges me back into the pleasure zone of serving You, where I'm reminded that what I do does, in fact, matter. Thank You for igniting again and again and again my longing to create a safe and warm and inviting place in our services where individuals can find hope in You and mending for their broken lives. Don't we all—stage people, booth people, pew people—need a place where we can enjoy community and worship You, You in all Your sovereignty and splendor?*

"This," I say to no one in the room, "is why we do what we do."

I lift my head and am keenly aware, even through tear-clouded eyes, of how drab and flat and uninviting the stage looks. Our team hung new, crisp, white fabric along the back wall just yesterday, but still, before me there is only dull and dingy and blah.

In one hour's time, though—thankfully—Wes will arrive with a smile on his face and color gels at his command. He will program lights to correspond to the layers of each song, such that when reflective choruses build to their crescendo, the lights do too.

He proves the point that worship leadership happens from places besides center stage. When he brings up strong, vibrant colors, worshippers experience God's majesty in gold, red, and orange. When a dose of gentleness is required, hues of blue and green wash across the stage like a gentle summer rain. Racing minds slow, heart rates fall, spirits calm, peace is made manifest right before our eyes.

I focus in on the full-size fichus hugging the drum kit and make a mental note for later to dust it and reposition it under the light. Over the years, numerous props have been added to the stage décor, just to keep things interesting. Candle walls, plants, fabric, various other wall displays, you name it. Whenever a new idea for set design would come to me, I'd say to the team, "You know, I've been thinking …" which always made them scatter.

They know, of course, that what always follows is laborious, tedious, costly, and necessitating at least six trips to The Home Depot. Food works wonders, though, and after a little Carl's Jr.-infused coaxing, my team mysteriously is ready to shop. Just one of the thousand things I love about leading this particular group of people. *Who is as blessed as I am, God? You are a good—no, a very good—God.*

I move to the edge of the cushioned bench and place my folded arms over the back of the pew in front of me, when it occurs to me that I am not alone. Instinctively, I look to my left, then to my right, before realizing my company isn't visible. God is the one who is here with me … God, who is just waiting.

He was present when I first walked in, of course, the dark and seemingly empty room already occupied with the presence of Light and Abundance Himself. He was waiting. He *is* waiting. For the artists, the pastors, the volunteers, the believers, the unconvinced, *all* of us. Weekend after weekend, I've asked Him to show up and move in the lives of those coming through our doors. And weekend after weekend, He has already been right here. Just waiting for *us* to show up.

My revelation is interrupted by the piercing creak of the wooden door swinging open. A facilities team member stands in the jam, clearly startled by my solo presence in the shadows. He asks if I'm okay. I make up something about needing to catch my breath for a few minutes before rehearsal starts, which evidently is enough information to throw him off the scent. I rise to my feet and head toward the booth as two staff members come barreling out from backstage, laughing and teasing and totally oblivious to the peace and quiet surrounding them. With that, the moment has officially passed.

Songs, prayer, transition, Scripture reading, drama, greeting, another transition, teaching, more songs, closing. I review each service component, ensuring things are correctly noted on the run sheet. The actors will arrive shortly to rehearse downstairs before they're scheduled onstage. *Make sure their lavs are ready.* I tick through my checklist, now wishing my mind were a little speedier, a tad more efficient. *Where did the time go?* Mental notes fly in from all sides, sticking to my brain like giant yellow sticky notes armed with a double layer of adhesive. *The band needs to run through extra transitions during rehearsal. There were fuzzy areas during that last run-through Thursday.* Load DVDs. *Check.* Add additional passage to the

PowerPoint sermon slides. *Check.* Reprint notes-view and let the other campus know the new version is ready to be loaded on their computer. *Check.* Place a fresh order of service on everyone's music stand and remember to point out the song-order change. *Check.* Clean up the empty water bottles onstage. Dust fichus. *Check, check.* Load the center-screen graphics. *Check.*

My list dwindles down as the room volume goes up. The electric guitar and bass players have arrived and are making their way to the stage to patch in and begin rehearsing their riffs. *Are they playing different songs?* How each one can hear himself in the midst of such chaos, I don't know. But now is not the time for me to probe.

I notice our computer operator has arrived; soon, the video screens come to life as she begins double-checking the lyrics to the songs. Wes walks in, and within mere moments, the once-drab stage is now drenched in deep color.

One by one, my teammates keep coming—band members, techs, vocalists—turning the once-silent space into a cacophony of sound. I glance at the clock and then back to the stage to take a quick assessment of who is here, who is missing. Piano, bass, electric, acoustic, violinist, keyboard—yep. Drummer? No dice. Worship leader? Really, now, is it asking too much to have our worship leader at preservice rehearsal? I pick up my ringing cell phone and learn that he got stuck in the Starbucks drive-through but is in the parking lot right now. He waltzes through the door before I can hang up, not a care in the world, and takes his position onstage.

We're now running seven minutes late, and still, no drummer. Musicians!

Thinking it's probably a good time to pray, I get everyone's attention and ask our guitarist to focus our attention on the One who we're really playing for. I'm distracted from what I'm sure is a meaningful prayer by the sound of our beloved drummer rushing through the doorway, tiptoeing down the center aisle, and crawling up onto his drum platform. He makes eye contact with me and shrugs his shoulders, as if to say, "Is tardiness really so bad? I have other fine qualities … really!" I think I'm the only one who has noticed his entry until his elbow accidentally crashes the cymbal and the whole team glares his way. Well, at least now we can start rehearsal.

For the next sixty minutes, the band plays various portions of songs until the worship leader is satisfied. Then, we connect with our other campus to fine-tune each transition. The actors make their way upstairs, pick up their mics, and head for the stage. Sound checks are conducted, light cues are reviewed, and then the room falls silent just before they begin to perform.

It's a powerful script that seems to hit each member of our team in a uniquely personal way. I feel a dose of enthusiasm well up in my spirit—*How will the congregation react to this? I wonder what God's going to do!*

I am snapped out of the moment by the arrival of our video directors and camera operators. *Have they gone over tonight's service? I hope they're ready.* The team takes their respective places, and we do a complete run-through to detect any last minute changes that must be made. Everything runs smoothly, so we close in prayer, clear the auditorium, and head backstage for some food.

The lighting is reduced to a warm glow; announcements scroll on the screens, and one by one, candles are lighted while music fills the air. Doors open, and people begin to arrive, some taking their seats immediately; others milling about to catch up on the week's goings-on with close friends and family members.

Ten minutes later, I put on my headset and test the connection to the video director and producer at the campus across town. T-minus five minutes, and the team takes their spots. Immediately at the top of the hour, I give the cue that officially starts the worship service. It's a moment that always conjures up images of King Hezekiah, the Old Testament king who played the producer role masterfully. Second Chronicles 29 (MSG) offers a marvelous picture of King Hezekiah "giving the signal to start" and then a whole slew of singers and musicians and congregants worshipping God for all they are worth. *What a sacred faith we have! What a sacred role I'm playing! What a sacred moment I'm experiencing!*

Sacred, that is, until the whole band grinds to a halt partway through the worship set.

It appears the worship leader has broken a guitar string, and instead of trying to finish the song, everyone onstage just stops and stares while their fearless leader switches to the backup guitar. Now, I should mention that, because of some nifty technology, we have an additional worship band at our satellite campus that was also playing along *live* and as I looked at my monitor I could see they had stopped as well. Our worship leader laughs and attempts to get the song going again and I, thinking how could I be helpful in a moment like this, decide to draw people's attention away from the fiasco onstage, by throwing one of our Scripture graphics onto the huge image magnification screen, by confidently hitting the Magic Button.

Sadly, though, I must have hit the wrong Magic Button, because all that appears on the screen behind our rattled band is that nice blue DVD-menu screen.

But our rehearsal went so smoothly!

You'd think that eventually things would simply straighten out—you know, the service would hop back on course, and the rest of the ninety-minute deal would be pretty uneventful—but no such luck.

I reengage in time to see one of our staff pastors take the stage in order to welcome the crowd, make a few announcements, and pray for our time together. It all goes fine until he forgets to tell the congregation to greet each other, which is really just a way of buying a few minutes for us to start the band's loop for a new worship song they're about to introduce. So, the well-meaning but unreliable staff pastor takes his seat, and the congregation stands there, eyes fixed on the stage folks, who have an unmistakable deer-in-the-headlights look on their faces. I toy around with the idea of calling "And … take two" on the house mic but settle for simply praying the ground will swallow me up whole instead.

Here, I think, is when you've got to give points for intent. I mean, to be fair, the worship leader didn't walk onstage that night thinking, *Hey, I think I'll break a string and throw the band totally off!* The staff pastor didn't maliciously neglect to have people greet each other. I certainly didn't plan to air the DVD-menu screen in all its glory.

Mishaps happen, no question about it. But in spite of our failures—or our successes, truth be told—the Spirit of God accomplishes exactly what He wants to accomplish, precisely when He wants to accomplish it.

As the offertory song unfolds, I find a minuscule pocket of air in which to breathe. On the center screen, stars are soaring through the galaxy while voices sing, "God of wonders beyond our galaxy, You are holy, holy! The universe declares your majesty...." Side screens reveal the lyrics, and even those who don't know the song by heart belt it out. Our bumpy start is somehow flowing into an easy rhythm. The collective emotion in the room has breadth and depth and, as a result of God's presence, soul. *Breathe, Cindy, breathe,* I exhort. *Give God room to work.*

The house lights dim as the service moves into a more reflective time of worship. The words "God is close at hand" fade up slowly on the center screen during a moving guitar solo. For the first time tonight, I notice the people who are sitting on the perimeter of the sound booth. *Look at their worshipful response! They are being touched by this service. It's so obvious....*

Some have their heads bowed. Some are standing with their arms raised. Others are sitting, watching, taking it all in. One lady in particular unknowingly beckons my attention as we begin singing about our deep desire for God's presence. She is seated to my right, her head down as if in prayer but not. She is wiping tears from her cheeks with both hands and softly rocking back and forth, back and forth, her own hands cradling her face and patiently catching every wet drop. *What is her story? Where is she from? What happened in her week? The tears ... what is troubling her so?*

I am captivated with her—faceless, nameless her—and with the unknowable journey she is on. *God, You see her face, You call her by name, You know every step. Let her know that You are enough....*

As the song continues, my eyes drift toward the stage. The sight catches my breath, floods my eyes with tears of my own. Every single band member, vocalist, worship leader is deeply engaged with this tender moment of worship. The one who continues to walk through the aftermath of a broken marriage has her left hand on the keyboard, the right lifted high in the air.

Every artist a worshipper. My heart swells.

The song winds down, the lights fade with the last note of the music, and the drama begins. Martha is frantic as she prepares for Jesus' arrival, while her sister, Mary, remains fixated on her single greatest desire: to sit at the feet of Jesus in order to know Him more. The "sisters" move through the scene, drawing in the audience with lines both humorous and harsh. The scene builds and builds, finally culminating with Martha's gut-wrenching realization that her priorities have been grossly out of whack. She grabs her sister by the shoulders and, with pleading eyes, begs an answer to her heart's deepest question: "Mary, what did I miss?! What did I miss?"

The air in the auditorium departs as Martha's words seep deeper into our consciousness. *What did I miss?* The lights fade to black as a single vocalist is heard from the stage. It's the type of moment that refuses to be programmed or written into a run sheet. It's a Spirit-moment—a slice in time when God shows up with powerful, obvious presence that engulfs every soul around. *Don't miss this!* God says to us all. *Don't miss Me.*

I see the woman to my right with head still bowed lift her eyes momentarily to stop the flow of tears. *God, touch her life and her heart, right here, right now. Please don't let her miss You.*

Our teaching pastor rises slowly, pausing before he utters a single word. Even then, not too quickly. Not too loudly. He's captured by the moment too, and his sensitivity to what is swirling all around is well placed. God is moving. Clearly, God is moving.

He prays. And when he's done, I exhale for the first time in six solid minutes. I push my shoulder blades back into my chair and rest in the belief that God must delight in artists' ability to usher in His presence. Despite our failings and flaws and broken guitar strings, He uses melody and harmony and instrumentation and drama and the spoken word to touch places unreachable by other more predictable, more controllable mediums.

The team convenes by the sound booth at the close of the service and laughs (sort of) about the fiasco that kicked things off tonight. I tell them of the tear-stained cheeks that had been to my right and how God chose to use even our imperfect acts of service to accomplish something profound in one woman's life.

I thank them for their hearts, their gifts, their time, their energies, and I urge them to get a good night's rest. "Let's be fresh and ready when we do it all again tomorrow morning," I say cheerfully. "Well, maybe we won't do *all* of it."

When the last piece of equipment has been shut off, I sit down for a moment on the very same pew I occupied earlier this morning and let my mind race through the fix-it routine it tends to entertain following each and every service. *What needs to happen before tomorrow's services? Where can we improve? What does the team need from me as their leader?*

Before I know it, the quiet overwhelms me once more. I look at the stage. Nothing. I listen for sound. Nothing.

Exactly one hour ago, this room was filled with a thousand people pouring out their hearts as perfect God collaborated with not-so-perfect artist.

Sixty minutes later, still He waits. *Are You always here? Do You promise to stay put till tomorrow's services?*

I hear teammates' voices from the hallway and know they'll come looking for me to walk me to my car. I bow my head and softly, audibly, say, "Thank You, Father. Thank You for touching me tonight. Thank You for pouring Your creativity into each one of us today as we stepped out to lead this congregation into Your presence. Thank You for the moments that refuse to be orchestrated, because they remind me each and every time that You are God and I am not. We are not. You are the Creator. You are the Producer. You are the Life-Changer. And here in this place—this otherwise soul-less room—You simply wait."

-10-

MINDING THE MOMENT

Saying Yes to God

Confirm God's invitation to you.... Don't put it off; do it now.
—2 PETER 1:10 MSG

THERE ARE ONE thousand four hundred and forty minutes in my day. I know this because my calculator and I sat down one afternoon and added it up. Arguably, it's a number that's rather fixed. But still, I used every ounce of my brain's creative juice to try to conjure up ways to change it. If only I could multiply my minutes, or at least make them slow down so I could (even once!) get through the day's to-do list. The *entire* list.

I'm sad to report it was wasted energy.

There's just no adding or stretching a single second. Despite my finest efforts, the clock extends no mercy. It keeps on ticking, whether I like it or not. One-one-thousand, two-one-thousand, three-one-thousand, four.... Within the framework of this incessant mechanical pulse, somewhere along life's path to mature adulthood I decided that if I couldn't increase my time, I'd just have to increase my pace.

For longer than I cared to admit, I'd rush to the shower, rush to get dressed, rush to work, rush to meet deadlines, rush home, rush to grab something for dinner, and then rush to bed, where I would tell myself to hurry up and go to sleep so I could repeat the routine again tomorrow—yet another day that was only going to allow me, you know, a mere one thousand four hundred and forty minutes.

All this rushing around would have been just fine, I suppose, except for the fact that a routine like this comes with some not-so-great side effects. Like numbness. Lack of creativity. Narrowed focus. Relational apathy. (Ask me how I know.) When I'm *really* in the zone, I can even add things like rage and resentment to the list.

I would get stressed out, frustrated, and ultracommitted to steamrolling anyone who was standing between the completion of my task and me. If and when I'd stop long enough to actually acknowledge the human beings to my right or to my left—typically, annoying types who claimed to have found something ridiculous like "balance" in life—I'd smile my best courtesy smile, nod my head as they told me their latest God-directed, people-intensive, life-giving adventure, and think to myself, *It truly does suck to be me.*

But that was the Me before the epiphany.

MINUTES VERSUS MOMENTS

On a warm and perfect Tuesday evening a few months ago, I pulled into the parking lot of my favorite Mexican-food restaurant, rolled down my windows, put my head back, and closed my eyes. For the umpteenth time, a few colleagues and I soon would be having a dinner/work-session over enchiladas and veggie quesadillas, but for now, it was just me, some downtime, and a little evening air.

As a gentle breeze blew through the truck, I brushed a few strands of hair away from my eyes and tried to block out all ambient noise from my consciousness—honking cars, wailing babies, the lively Latino beat blaring through the courtyard speakers. There was a lovely stream nearby, and so it became my sole aim to focus intently enough on the trickling water coming down in folds over the river rocks below that I could hear it and it alone.

Ten minutes into my self-induced state of calm, streams of water from my own two eyes vied for my attention. Sure, I could think of a half dozen places I'd rather be than at yet another dinnertime business meeting, but was I really this tired and deflated and close to the edge?

As I sat there silently convulsing, I wondered when was the last time I had taken a real break from the monotony of my world— *When did I last pack up the truck and head for the mountains, the happy place that beats all others?*

Lately, my schedule had been a nonstop run on a gerbil's wheel. I got up, got ready, got in the truck, and went to work. With almost no assistance from me, it seemed, my SUV would drive me right to the church, where I'd go through a full day of meetings, interventions, and inquisitions. Hours later, weary and bleary and oblivious to the fact that I hadn't seen the sun all day, I'd climb back into my vehicle and head home.

Day after day after day, this was the sum total of my existence.

As a staff, we were in yet another so-called "season of

transition," one that demanded reserves of strength, energy, and
time I simply didn't possess. Add to that worship services that
rolled around week after week after week (uncanny, the regular-
ity!), and it seemed there was no way out.

Sitting there outside that Mexican-food restaurant, I picked
apart my day-by-day life, my heart sinking a little more with each
realization.

Mondays were technically my days "off," except for the fact that,
thanks to cell phones and e-mail, it seemed I was perpetually "on."
In between returning messages, Mondays also meant catching up
on household chores, paying bills, and buying groceries. Tuesdays
were staff-team-meeting days. Also the day I was to catch up on
anything left over from the previous weekend of worship services.
Wednesdays meant staff chapel, Executive Council leadership team
meetings, worship planning meetings, and other mind-numbing
and morale-busting energy expenses. Thursdays meant more meetings … as well as band and vocal rehearsals in the evening hours.
Fridays were for finishing designing graphics for the weekend services, locating Bible verses to support each song, and touching base
with the team to confirm any last-minute changes. Saturdays? I'd
arrive early in the morning, finish up the stage design, work with
the lighting coordinators, oversee rehearsal, do a clean run-through
with band members and vocalists, and then produce one of the
three weekend worship services. Finally, there was Sunday. Sundays
meant yet another early arrival, finalizing changes from the night
before, producing the other two services, and, sometime around
two in the afternoon, heading home to collapse on the couch.

What kind of life was this, really?

The question was rhetorical, but still, I answered. *Pathetic, that's what kind.*

In between my other usual leadership chores like resolving budget matters, reviewing résumés, hunting for the perfect song for the next Communion service, and trying desperately to remember to pick up dog food for my oft-neglected golden retriever, (*someone* in my house should be eating regularly), I questioned God.

Had He blinked and forgotten me? Had He lost my file? Were my needs so petty that I got parked on permanent hold, while He sorted out other, more pressing issues?

Perhaps this is precisely what had happened, which is why I decided to help Him out a little—maybe take matters into my own hands for a spell. Give the Guy a break, you know … something for which I was sure He'd be eternally grateful. (Given His eternal nature, He really *could* thank me for that long.)

And that's where the whole rushing thing had begun. I had put myself on automatic pilot and nuzzled up closer to my friends Predictability and Familiarity and Speed, closing myself off from humankind and training my eyes instead on the mighty to-do list. I was bound and determined to be the picture of productivity, the envy of type-As worldwide. Maybe if I never slowed down, I reasoned, I'd never have to look my vacuous life in the face.

You're missing the moment.

"Huh?"

Cindy, you're missing the moment.

Somewhere between the trickling drops running off the stream—not to mention my face—came those words, etched as if by an engraver's tool carving deep into the recesses of my soul. They were spoken gently, in a matter-of-fact sort of way, completely devoid of condemnation or critique. And in my heart, I knew exactly where they came from. The "voice," if you will, was God's—unmistakably. He was the one who could see past the robotic me, the me who was taking shelter in my ridiculous routine.

God must have known all along that my feeble attempts to "help Him out" were really just veiled attempts to bring Him down to my level so that I could control Him ... as if that were possible. As the truth of His words found their sticking place, a deep sense of regret washed over me. When had I become Martha, the same Martha that had been portrayed in that months-ago drama, right on our own church's stage?

Oh, God, what did I miss?

What did I miss when I was plowing ahead—ahead of You, ahead of everyone around me, ahead of myself? What creative idea did I not implement? What life transformation did I refuse to observe? What truth did I skirt? What did I miss?

It was an a-ha that would completely change the way I approached my days—the days that were once made up of minutes would now be made up of *moments*, "God-moments," I decided then and there, that I would henceforth refuse to miss.

WHAT JESUS KNEW OF GOD-MOMENTS

During His time here on planet Earth, Jesus set the perfect example for us to follow regarding marking time by moments rather than minutes. He knew time on earth was fleeting and therefore gave careful thought to when to be fully present and when to pull back, when to be quiet and when to speak, when to subvert His day's agenda and take a detour instead. He knew the value of the God-moment and never missed a single one.

If I was ever going to step off the gerbil wheel, I needed to learn how to allow my heart to embrace unexpected God-moments too, those unplanned, unstructured, uncontrollable occasions when God effects marvelous change in my life or in the life of someone I know. So, that's what I set out to do.

I gave it a few minutes of thought, this question of what did Jesus understand about "God-moments" that allowed Him to live in a meaningful way instead of rushing around like a madman every-day? Three themes came to mind. Far from an exhaustive list, at least it gave me a few hooks to hang onto as I forged ahead with this new life-strategy. First, Jesus seemed to "get" the fact that not every single minute of every single day equated to a powerful "God-moment." Second, He knew that saying yes to a God-moment always meant saying no to something else. And third, He knew that there was always more to God-moments than what meets the eye.

Not Every Minute Is a Moment

We all have normal day-to-day responsibilities that have to be met, lest we wind up on the street holding Will Sing for Food signs (or Paint or Dance or Act). The vast majority of people do not have the luxury of orchestrating every day of life to reflect only the things they love the most. Painters pay bills. Writers buy groceries. Vocalists pick up the dry cleaning. Drummers ... well, they really do just drum all day long, but that's the exception to my point, not the rule.

There are days when I sit in my office feeling no more useful than one of those Crazy 8 balls with the weird fluid inside. You think up a question, shake the ball for a bit, and then, poof! Some arbitrary answer to your life's most pressing query floats to the surface. In my context, a staff member enters my office, poses a question, shakes me a little, and poof! I dole out an arbitrary answer before calling "Next!" to contestant number two, who is waiting patiently in the hallway.

Suffice it to say, doing a Crazy 8 impersonation is not a favorite part of my job. I'd much rather spend 100 percent of my time engaging in philosophical discussions about art and church and creativity, or releasing artists to pursue their God-given talents, or dreaming bigger dreams for how Christ-followers can reach those not yet persuaded to follow Christ through mediums like paint and song and dance.

But decisions have to get made. Expenses have to get accounted for. Phone calls have to get returned. The administrative stuff of life has to get done.

Toilets don't clean themselves, you know.

Jesus knew this. (I'm talking here about the administrative stuff, not necessarily the toilets.) He knew that He couldn't spend twenty-four hours a day doing only what He loved—teaching and healing and doting on humankind. He also had to do the hard work of casting vision and training disciples and resolving internal disputes. I'm sure there were many days when His minutes couldn't tick by fast enough, for all the monotony and frustration they held. We'll have days like that too—it's a reality we can't control.

What we *can* control is our ability to stay wildly open to the times when God-moments peek through.

Embracing the Moment Is a Decision

God-moments are always unplanned, unexpected, and quite sudden. When one decides to present itself, you and I have a quick decision to make: Will we engage, or will we tell God He'll have to come back later, we're far too busy to be interrupted right now?

Jesus was the master at getting this decision right. He'd shirk duty to play with a few kids, push pause on His agenda to ask a heartfelt question of someone who was hurting, or, even after a wearying day's journey, take the long way home if it meant enfolding an outsider with a dose of community. Saying yes to God-moments meant, on occasion, saying no to what was planned, intended, or expected of Him—something that, a couple of weeks ago, I decided to try.

A couple of close friends had asked me over for dinner, and I had said yes. (Who refuses a home-cooked meal?) When the day arrived, though, I was busy writing this particular chapter. For a split second, I was tempted to call them and ask if we could reschedule. I was on deadline, after all, and I'd given my word to my publisher. But I'd also given my word to this couple. How ironic it would be, I finally concluded, for me to neglect what was probably a God-moment in the making in order to stay home and write about not neglecting God-moments.

I shut the lid on my laptop, refreshed my makeup, and headed to their home for what would prove to be a wonderful evening of food, laughter, and mutual encouragement. I left my home stressed but their home blessed. Isn't that just like God?

There's More Here Than Meets the Eye

Jesus also knew God-moments carried realities and implications invisible to the naked eye. A meal shared could hold greater meaning than mere meat and potatoes. A kind word offered could hold greater importance than the audible syllables exchanged. A touch extended, greater power. A thoughtful question, greater substance. A prayer prayed, greater impact.

In recent months, I've experienced countless God-moments where the more-than-meets-the-eye reality played out just this way. One of them happened around the dining-room table at Dan and Shirley's house, two of my friends and beloved partners in ministry. Dan is a chaplain in a high security prison and was recounting the story for me of an inmate named Chuck who was a fabulous musician and a Christ-follower who was still trying to find his way. As I took in the details of Chuck's life, something inside of me told me to pay closer attention to what I was hearing. It was obvious that Dan loved Chuck like a father loves a son and was doing everything possible to help Chuck progress along his spiritual and artistic journeys alike. Chuck had recently asked Dan if he thought there ever would be a way for his life inside a prison cell to "impact the outside world." It was obvious Chuck wanted to touch others' lives. But how do you do that when you're locked away?

Like a bolt of lightning, God gave me a staggering idea. I rested my fork on the side of my plate, wiped my mouth with the corner of my napkin, and said, "Dan, do you think I could meet your friend Chuck?"

Dan grinned. "I already told him about you and about our church and about our emphasis on the power of 'story.' He's more than a little excited to talk with you!"

Plans were immediately under way, and five weeks later, I found myself standing in the same room as Chuck. He warmly grasped my hand, took a deep breath, and said, "Cindy, it's nice to meet you. Thank you for coming." Based on the way he hung back with Dan, I knew I wasn't the only one who was nervous. We both felt trepidation—I wondered what questions I would ask, and he wondered why I'd bother to listen to his replies.

Over the next two and a half hours, Chuck and I sat across from each other with cameras rolling and Dan standing by, the only sound in the small prison chapel the rising and falling of each of our voices.

I asked about Chuck's childhood, about his family, and about his favorite things to do when he was a kid. He talked about growing up in the church, his blossoming love for music and playing the drums at the early age of three. It all seemed so normal. So predictable. So good. And yet there was a reason we were conducting the interview from the inside of a prison. Something had happened in this man's life that was going to change everything forever.

"Chuck," I finally said, after taking a deep breath, "given where you and I are seated today, I have to ask you about 'that' day. Can you tell me what happened?"

He nodded his head in agreement, as if conceding the point that he owed the question an answer. Then he stared at the floor, heavy silence surrounding us. Minutes went by, and then finally, he spoke. "The day started like any other. But … well, there was an argument. There was a gun in the room. Shots were fired. And in the end … someone's life was taken."

As tears rolled down Chuck's cheeks, he continued telling me his story—about the trial, about the sentencing, about finding himself at the age of sixteen walking through the gates of prison. "What am I supposed to do with you?" the warden would say. "You're just a boy." Most friends Chuck's age were grinning for their driver-license photo around the time he was put away. But for Chuck, there were no smiles to be found.

Even from behind bars, Chuck's love for music flourished. He learned to play new instruments—the keyboard, the bass guitar—and began to write new songs. God had been a thing of his past until his sister challenged him to reconsider. Slowly but deliberately, Chuck began to go God's way with his life. He might be bound to a cell, but he would know freedom in Christ.

My team and I filmed the balance of Chuck's story, as well as him strumming and singing two of his original songs, before we began to shut down our interview. I would walk out of prison that day unsure of how or when his story would be used "outside of prison," as he had wondered. Still, it was a tale I knew would be told.

Several days after the interview with Chuck, our pastor said that he would soon be introducing a four-part series based on Isaiah 61. The key verse he wanted to focus on says, "The Spirit of the

Sovereign LORD is on me, because the LORD has anointed me to preach good news to the poor. He has sent me to bind up the brokenhearted, to proclaim freedom for the captives and release from darkness for the prisoners" (v. 1).

Freedom for the captives. There it was, God's answer to my question about how Chuck's story would be shared.

My team and I edited our interview with Chuck and then aired it during four powerful weekend services that centered on the theme of setting bound-up captives free. That weekend, I watched as more than five thousand attendees engaged with a story beyond their own. As the DVD rolled, I witnessed an incarcerated young man encouraging the "free" among us to grasp the reality that "our chains are gone, and we have been set free" when we truly seek the freedom found in Christ and Christ alone.

Chuck is one of the most talented artists I have ever known. He has grown into an incredible worship leader who leads hundreds of men who have committed crimes too hard to comprehend in worship. God is using Chuck's "yes"—his talents and his heart— to lead in God-charged life-changing moments even from behind a fortified set of prison walls.

To think that the whole deal—the interview, the airing, the life change that occurred as a result—could be traced back to a *single* moment around Dan and Shirley's dining-room table ... it was almost too much to bear. These are the moments I pray I will *always* mind.

THE MOMENT IS NOW

In *The Traveler's Gift*, author Andy Andrews writes about a room called "Never Was."[1] It's a giant warehouse of a room that holds all of the things God was ready to deliver to people, had they only persevered in prayer a moment longer.

I read the story again recently, this time imagining a room of God's called "Never Created."

What if in that room sat billions of blank canvases, each with its own vision of what it was to be, if only someone had painted it? What if the corner held a pile of dusty ballet shoes, sad and despondent over their never-choreographed dances? What if floating around the ceiling were lyrics to never-sung worship songs? What if lines of unread scripts bounced around waiting to take their cue onstage? What if blocks of clay sat, longing for the hands of potters to address their never-formed state? What if never-written books lined shelf after shelf, their wordless pages just waiting for stories and adventures and truth?

I thought about the terrible, terrible room called "Never Created" and felt a quickening in my pulse, a strengthening resolve in my heart to challenge artists of all disciplines to create! And to create now. One of my favorite authors, Madeleine L'Engle, once wrote that, "The artist must be obedient to the work ... I believe that each work of art, whether it is a work of great genius, or something very small, comes to the artist and says, 'Here I am. Enflesh me. Give birth to me.' And the artist either says, 'My soul doth magnify the Lord,' and willingly becomes the bearer of the work, or refuses."[2]

The artist either displays God's splendor and beauty, or else refuses.

The artist either creates from the soul, or else refuses.

The artist either exercises spiritual disciplines, or else refuses.

Takes risks, or else refuses.

Loves from the depths of the heart, or else refuses.

Fans the flames of their God-given gifts, or else refuses.

Leads others toward their "yes," or else refuses.

The artist either seizes God-moments, or else refuses.

The moment is now, artist. I wonder, how will you respond?

POSTSCRIPT

MY FRIEND ROBIN delivered a healthy baby boy a few years ago, and I had the high honor of standing right by her side as Micah arrived. It was a perfect and wonderful experience on a perfect and wonderful day. During the nine months prior to that, though, things weren't always so perfect and wonderful. On more than a few occasions, Robin's usually-elated emotional state plummeted into a pit of terrific fear: "I can't do this," she'd say. "Really."

When the call came the morning of Micah's birth—"Cindy, we're headed to the hospital! It's time."—I had my own *I can't do this* moment. I had never been inside of a delivery room. I did not like hospitals. And I felt sure the perfect storm of metal instruments and blood and people experiencing lots of pain would be my ultimate undoing.

A few hours later, though, when Micah first tested his baby-lungs and wailed his face into a perfect interpretation of a prune, we *all* forgot those things we couldn't do, Aunt Cindy included, and joyously welcomed the new little life into the world.

This manuscript is my Micah.

I watched an interview with Amy Grant on TV right before her book came out, and I was struck by the fact that the singer/songwriter had all of a sudden become an author. She said that she thought *everyone* should write, because it was in the writing of life that you really come to value it. Those were profound words to me. And although writing has never been my strong suit, her exhortation kind of put me on the hook. For the past five years, in fact, I've known that getting some of the lessons I've learned down on paper—writing a bona fide *book*—was something God was asking me to do. Clearly. Unapologetically. And with annoying persistence.

But I can't do this, God, I'd think. *Really!*

Twelve months ago, still feeling wobbly and inadequate, I began the mind-numbingly lovely process of writing this book. I told God that in exchange for following orders about the book thing, I now had a favor to ask of Him. "Please allow me to *live* every chapter as I *write* it."

I thought this seemed like a very noble prayer, and so I prayed it diligently, most every day I could remember to do so. Little did I know just how faithful God would be to take my request seriously.

I'd sit down to begin a new chapter and feel that awful welling up of fear as the blank screen and blinking cursor mocked me with the reminder that they were ready when I was. (*Oh, shut up!* I would think every time.)

Later, when I'd actually completed the chapter and hit Send to my editor, I would realize that the tears and laughter and agony and poured-out, Spirit-enabled thoughts were all worth it, because the pages I had written really did reflect the truth of who I am, the truth of what I have experienced thus far, the truth of how I have led. The net effect was a stripped-bare, completely depleted version of me I've known only once, maybe twice, in my entire life, but if the by-product would give artists and leaders of artists a little hope, a little insight, a little encouragement, then I'd gladly do it all over again, no questions asked.

As an artist, I am changed. As an author, I am humbled. And as a Christ-follower, I am more in love with my God than ever before. The book is done. And facing my greatest fear—baring my soul on paper this way—has afforded me priceless and intimate moments with my Creator, the kind that are so weightless and fragile and otherworldly that you're sure if you blink or twitch or breathe a little too deeply, you'll frighten them away.

It has been in *those* moments that, like Micah's declaration that he was officially here, I have known God's here-ness too. I have felt the closeness of His breath and heard the beat of His heart and sensed the tenderness in His voice—all realities that make anxiety attacks *far* more tolerable, if you ask me.

I'm convinced that when I'm ninety-five, I'll look up from my rocker on the porch of the artist's nursing home I've built and know beyond the shadow of a doubt that this project—this simple collection of chapters—most accurately defines and demonstrates who I am.

And for the opportunity to say yes to creating it, God knows I am grateful.

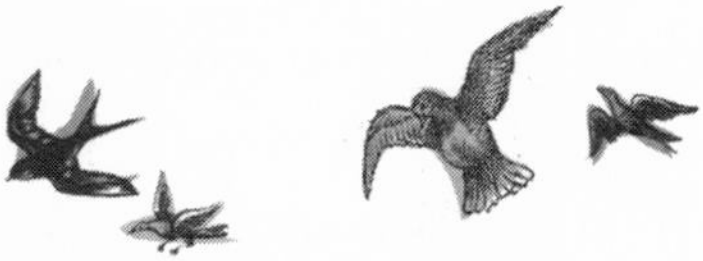

NOTES

Chapter 1
1. Henri Nouwen, *The Return of the Prodigal Son* (New York: Doubleday, 1992), 10. This is a prime example of how art begets art. I urge you to read his book and then create from what it stirs within you.
2. Ibid.

Chapter 2
1. Anne Lamott, *Grace (Eventually): Thoughts on Faith* (New York: Riverhead, 2007), 28–29.
2. Pope John Paul II, *Letter to Artists* (Chicago: Archdiocese of Chicago Liturgy Training Publications, 1999).

Chapter 3
1. Should I ever doubt the impact our gallery has, here's one of many great encouragements received by a member of our congregation:

From: Suzanne
Sent: Mon 8/20/2007 11:20 AM
To: Cindy West
Subject: Thank you!
Cindy, My girls and I came in through the west door of the sanctuary and we lingered in that hallway as we looked at the paintings hung there. What a great way to start a Sunday morning. I enjoyed reading the artists' bios and then thought about what it means to worship as I was looking upon the art I saw. My thoughts definitely followed a different path than was customary ... all good. Please give my thanks to the all who are involved with submitting, hanging, and showing the wonderful art from season to season!
God is good.

Chapter 4

1. Oswald Chambers, "The Inspiration of Spiritual Initiative," *My Utmost for His Highest,* www.rbc.org/devotionals/my-utmost-for-his-highest/02/16/devotion. aspx?year=2008 (accessed May 9, 2008).
2. Gordon MacKenzie, *Orbiting the Giant Hairball* (New York: Penguin, 1998), 224 (italics added). (All artists should have this book in their creative library!)
3. C. S. Lewis, *The Problem of Pain* (New York: HarperCollins, 1996), 91.

Chapter 5

1. Francis Schaeffer, *Art and the Bible* (Downers Grove, IL: InterVarsity, 1973), 33.
2. If you've never walked through a Spiritual Gifts Assessment, I encourage you to pick up *S.H.A.P.E. Finding and Fulfilling Your Unique Purpose for Life* by Eric Rees.
3. Jim Krause, *Creative Sparks* (Cincinnati, OH: HOW Design Books, 2003), 110. Get this book and put it on your shelf for the days when your creativity might be in the fog or you find yourself on dry ground. I promise it will inspire you!
4. Krause, *Creative Sparks,* 110.
5. Merriam-Webster Online, www.merriam-webster.com (accessed May 9, 2008).
6. "More of You" © 2007 Mark Tedder.
7. Mark Galli, *Francis of Assisi and His World, from the Third Letter to the Agnes of Prague, 1238* (Oxford, England: Lion Hudson, 2002), 110.
8. See also 1 Corinthians 13:12: "Now we see but a poor reflection as in a mirror; then we shall see face to face. Now I know in part; then I shall know fully, even as I am fully known." What an incredible promise to hang onto when bed-head overtakes my view.

Chapter 6

1. "Convening with the Enemy," *SEEN: The Journal of CIVA.* Vol. 12, 2006.

Chapter 8

1. Pope John Paul II, *Letter to Artists.*
2. Rory Noland, *The Heart of the Artist* (Grand Rapids, MI: Zondervan, 1999).

Chapter 10

1. Andy Andrews, The Traveler's Gift (Nashville, TN: Thomas Nelson, 2002), 157.
2. Madeleine L'Engle, *Walking on Water, Reflections on Faith and Art* (Colorado Springs: WaterBrook), 17.

To contact Cindy,
go to isayyes.net.